AGAINST ALL ODDS

Against All Odds

Scott Schaeffer-Duffy

Haley's
Athol, Massachusetts

© 2025 by Scott Schaeffer-Duffy

All rights reserved. With the exception of short excerpts in a review or critical article, no part of this book may be re-produced by any means, including information storage and retrieval or photocopying equipment, without written permission of the publisher, Haley's.

Haley's
488 South Main Street
Athol, MA 01331
haley.antique@verizon.net
978.249.9400

Cover design by Aiden Duffy.

Copy edited by Debra Ellis.

International Standard Book Number, trade paperback: 978-1-956055-32-0

International Standard Book Number, hardcover: 978-1-956055-33-7

International Standard Book Number, watermarked pdf: 978-1-956055-34-4

Library of Congress Control Number: 2025942475

:

for my beloved grandchildren
May, Frances, Theo, Fiona, Isaiah, and Aya

May they enjoy a world without nuclear weapons

Persistence is the Mother of good luck.
—an Irish proverb

Contents

Why Against All Odds? 1
Tom Lewis 3
The Eyes, Ears, and Brains of Armageddon 7
Inch by Inch 9
First Civil Disobedience 15
Shareholder Activism 21
A Stronger Approach 23
The Walls of Jericho and More 29
Peace Pentecost, 1983 32
Good Friday, 1984. 33
Hiroshima Day 1984. 41
A Parental Appeal and More. 52
Forty-Day Preparation for More Civil Disobedience 55
Unexpected Consequences 62
Valentine's Day Reimagined 80
Solitary Witness 84
More Lovers 86
The Last Civil Disobedience. 95
What Did the Workers Think? 103
The Work Goes On. 109
In Blessed Memory. 111
About the Author 113
Colophon 115

Illustrations

Tom Lewis	3
Catonsville Nine	5
"Sunflower"	6
MX nuclear missile with components made by GTE	8
Matt Shorten	11
vigiler at GTE	12
Sster Clare Carter, Hattie Nestel, and Sandra Lett	14
Father Leo Barry and Father Bernie Gilgun	14
Members of Noonday Catholic Worker Farm of Winchendon, Massachusetts, and Worcester's Olive Branch Community	15
Margie Farren, Scott Duffy, Tom Doughton, Tom Lewis Celia Jesa-Ivy, and Ray Demers	17
"Jail Cell"	19
"My Feet"	20
"GTE Shareholders Convene"	22
"Dr. Sandra O. Moose, GTE Board Member"	22
MX Peace Witness group at Westborough District Court	23
Scott Schaeffer Duffy kneels in the GTE yard	24
antibomb protesters picket at GTE plant	29
flag-waving marchers emulate Israelites bringing down walls of Jericho	30
"What the hell are we gonna do?"	30
Sue Malone, Michael True, Mary Laurel True, Tom Lewis, Claire Schaeffer, Scott Duffy, and Dan Lawrence	33
Westborough Police arrest Sue Malone at GTE	35
police arrest Claire Schaeffer, left, and Michael True at GTE	36
Dan Lawrence and Tom Lewis arrive at court	37
Dan Lawrence folds a prayerful banner	40
1984 GTE ad	45

illustrations continued on page xii

illustrations continued from page xi

Ernestine LeBeau, Tom Lewis, Scott Schaeffer-Duffy, and Claire Schaeffer-Duffy	49
Eight witness at GTE on Good Friday, 1985	58
Dan Sicken, Father Bob Branconnier, and Claire Schaeffer-Duffy listen during arraignment	59
Father Bob Branconnier celebrates Mass	61
Paul Giamo, GTE Officer Michael Augustine, and Connie Riley	63
GTE security officer arrests Scott Schaeffer-Duffy	64
Deirdre Doran and Mary Jane Rosati serve sentences in Framingham	74
Daniel Sicken and Paul Giaimo serve time at Worcester County Jail	75
Carol Bellin and Scott Schaeffer-Duffy assert that love disarms	80
GTE employee cleans blood from company sign	81
Scott Schaeffer-Duffy and Carol Bellin wait in court lobby	82
GTE workers in office cubicles	84
Officer Paul Donnelly escorts Dan Ethier into court	85
a police officer bars Dan Lawrence and Scott Schaeffer-Duffy	87
police arrest Dan Lawrence, Deidre Nuñez, and Clare Grady	88
invitation to their trial	95
Hattie Nestel, Jennifer Hoffman, Ken Synan, Tom Lewis, and Scott Schaeffer-Duffy	97
drawing by Tom Lewis depicting the homeless	98
Hattie Nestel, Michel Cahill, and Jennifer Hoffman	100
Scott Schaeffer-Duffy and Ken Synan	100
Scott and Claire Schaeffer-Duffy	106

In Blessed Memory

Tom Lewis	111
Peter DeMott	111
Sue Malone	111
Margie Farren	111
Father Bernie Gilgun	111
Barbara Roberts	111
Michael True	111
Scott Schaeffer-Duffy biography photo	113

Why Against All Odds?

As corporations and governments grow more powerful, the notion that an individual or even a group of individuals could persuade either institution to abandon a financially profitable, but genocidal, course of action seems less and less likely. While a skinny teenager named David defeated the giant Goliath, the probability that today's underdogs can beat global behemoths is minuscule.

And yet, that is precisely the kind of story *Against All Odds* conveys.

David achieved victory with a single swing of his slingshot, but most empires do not fall as easily. A mighty corporation with the full financial and political backing of the US government to build an advanced nuclear weapons guidance system could not be quickly disarmed, especially not at the height of the Cold War during the eight-year presidency of Ronald Reagan. So preposterous is the notion that the military-industrial complex could be thwarted by grass roots activists that it would require multiple miracles as rare as the ground ball going through Bill Buckner's legs in Game 6 of the 1986 World Series, which saw the underdog New York Mets steal the crown. And yet, those once-in-a-lifetime events occur in *Against All Odds*.

While my devoted spouse likes to deride my first book, *Nothing Is Impossible,* as truth's distant cousin, a characterization I vigorously contest, *Against All Odds* includes meticulous documentation. Sources include books, newspaper articles, editorials, letters, input from those quoted, and the author's personal experience. Thankfully, the Truth—with a capital T in this case—happens to be enormously varied, inspiring, informative, and often quite funny.

You may well ask, "What possible relevance could a campaign from the era of rotary phones and eight-track tapes have today?" I contend that the specific tactics may be out of date, but the creativity, persistence, spirituality, and community out of which they arose is timeless. The people on the front lines of today's battles against racism, sexism, poverty, war, nuclear weapons, and artificial intelligence, not to mention the urgency of stemming the climate emergency, need to recall stories—like the Boston Red Sox coming back from a three-game deficit to defeat the New York Yankees on the way to their first World Series victory in eighty-six years—to give them hope. That's exactly what *Against All Odds* carries: a boatload of hope.

Tom Lewis

The story of Tom Lewis begins at a carnival. In 1963, a twenty-three-year-old Catholic artist named Thomas Patrick Lewis went to the gate of the segregated Gwynn Oak Amusement Park outside Baltimore where he planned to sketch civil rights demonstrators. As Tom stood on the sidelines, he became uncomfortable with racist catcalling from spectators standing around him. In what he later described as the most terrifying act of his entire life, Tom put his sketch pad into his bag, picked up a sign, and joined the protesters. He later said, "It is a shocking thing walking a picket line for the first time sensing the hostility of the White people."

Tom Lewis smiles in 2004 next to one of his award-winning paintings at Fitchburg Art Museum.
photo courtesy of *Worcester Telegram & Gazette*

After joining the Catholic Interracial Council and the Congress of Racial Equality, both organizations promoting civil rights for all Americans, Tom and another friend checked out an apartment for rent in Timonium, Maryland. Tom told the landlord, "The place looks great. Our third housemate should arrive shortly. If he likes it, too, we'll rent it." When a Black man arrived as the third potential renter, the owner refused to rent to them. Tom and his two companions sat down, refused to leave, and were arrested in Tom's first act of nonviolent civil disobedience.

Like many civil rights activists, Tom came to oppose the Vietnam War early and often. In a group later called the Baltimore Four, Tom, Josephite priest Philip Berrigan, writer David Eberhardt, and US Air Force veteran and United Church of Christ pastor, Reverend James L. Mengel III poured their own blood on draft files on October 27, 1967, in the Baltimore Selective Service office to protest what Phil called "the pitiful waste of American and Vietnamese blood in Indochina."

While in lockup over the weekend before their Monday arraignment, Phil confessed to Tom that he wondered what more they could do to mobilize Catholics against the war. Tom suggested that, if they were released on personal recognizance, they do a more daring protest. And so, with six other Roman Catholics, Tom Melville, George Mische, Mary Moylan, Marjorie Bradford Melville, David Darst, and John Hogan, Phil and Tom planned to enter the selective service office in Catonsville, Maryland, take draft files into the parking lot, and burn them with homemade napalm, a deadly incendiary gas used by the American military against Vietnamese combatants and civilians.

Phil really hoped to convince his brother Daniel to join them. Daniel, a Jesuit priest, had just returned from a mission with Howard Zinn, a professor of history at Boston University, to North Vietnam to bring American prisoners of war home. Tom and Phil sat with Dan late into the night over a bottle of Irish whiskey until they resolved the matter.

Drawing on his experience in a Hanoi bomb shelter, Dan would later write:

> Our apologies, good friends, for the fracture of good order, the burning of paper instead of children, the angering of the orderlies in the front parlor of the charnel house. We could not, so help us God, do otherwise. For we are sick at heart, our hearts give us no rest for thinking of the Land of Burning Children.

A week after his arrest for what came to be known internationally as the Catonsville Nine, Tom went on trial with Phil, Eberhardt, and Mengel for the Baltimore Four protest. A jury convicted them all. The judge, who was angry that Phil had burned draft files at Catonsville while on bail, gave him the maximum sentence, six years in jail. But prior to Tom's sentencing, the judge asked if he had anything to say. When Tom said no, the judge repeated his question.

Tom replied, "No, your honor, I've said everything I need to say."

To Tom's surprise, the judge appealed a third time: "Are you absolutely sure, Mr. Lewis? This is your last chance to say anything before sentencing. Don't you have anything to say?"

Tom wondered why the judge was so insistent. He figured he was looking for some remark to justify giving Tom a more lenient sentence than he gave Phil, whom many considered the protest's ringleader. Tom therefore said, "Yes, your honor, since you ask. I do have a quote that is meaningful for me."

The judge leaned forward and said, "Yes, Mr. Lewis. Please proceed."

With all seriousness, Tom declared, "'You can lead a horse to water, but a pencil must be lead.' That's from Laurel and Hardy, your honor."

The judge thundered, "Is that part of your philosophy, too, Mr. Lewis? Six years!" Tom and Phil waited in jail until their trial for the draft-file burning began.

Dan Berrigan's 1970 play *The Trial of the Catonsville Nine* used trial transcripts to preserve the courtroom drama for posterity. Here are excerpts from Tom's testimony:

The Catonsville Nine hold hands, from left, including David Darst, Marjorie Melville, Tom Lewis, Father Philip Berrigan of the Congregation of Jesus and Mary, John Hogan, Tom Melville, Father Daniel Berrigan of the Society of Jesus, and Mary Moylan.
Baltimore Sun photo.

DEFENSE

What opinion did you come to with respect to the war in Vietnam?

THOMAS LEWIS

I came to the conclusion that the war is totally outrageous from the Christian point of view.

DEFENSE

On the strength of these beliefs, did you engage in peace activity?

THOMAS LEWIS

Yes, after the speech of Pope Paul at the UN (where the pontiff pleaded "Never again war!"), a group of us began what we called the Interfaith Peace Mission of Baltimore. We were a group of concerned people attempting to express to others what we felt about the war. We began with a peace vigil at one of the churches here. We prayed for peace in response to the invitation of religious leaders throughout the world. We followed this with a walk demonstrating visually our hope for peace. Things progressed. We had visits with Maryland congressmen and senators. We wrote letters to them and delivered them personally in Washington. We met with silence from all of them. We met with hostility and apathy. I then moved into civil disobedience.

Sunflower
14x40 inches
ink on rice paper by Tom Lewis

PROSECUTION

Yes or no, were you aware that it was against the law to take records from the selective service and burn them?

THOMAS LEWIS

I wasn't concerned with the law. I wasn't even thinking about the law. I was thinking what those records meant. I went in there with the intent of stopping what the files justify. The young men whose files we destroyed have not yet been drafted, may not be drafted, may not be sent to Vietnam for cannon fodder. My intent in going there was to save lives. A person may break the law to save lives.

JUDGE

If these men were not sent, other people would have been sent who would not otherwise have been sent, would they not?

THOMAS LEWIS

But why your honor? Why this? Why does it have to be like this? You are accepting the fact that if these men are not sent other men will be sent. You are not even asking what can be done to stop this insane killing. You are accepting this as in Nazi Germany people accepted the massacre of other people. This is insane. I protest this.

PROSECUTION

Your honor, I move that all of this be stricken. I don't know how long he is going to continue.

THOMAS LEWIS

How long? I have six years, Mr. Prosecutor. I have lots of time.

All nine defendants were convicted. Tom was sentenced to three and a half more years in jail for a total of nine and a half years. While doing time in Lewisburg, Pennsylvania, Federal Penitentiary, Tom perfected his self-definition as an artist-activist. He made paintings of inmates out of mayonnaise and other materials until he could get proper supplies. He did a series of woodcuts featuring sunflowers, an international symbol of disarmament, as well as a beautiful tree outside the prison yard.

After his release from prison after three and a half years and the end of the Vietnam War, Tom's activism flowed naturally into work for nuclear disarmament, a cause that Phil, Dan, and Tom knew deserved urgent attention. He moved to Worcester, Massachusetts, where he bought a three-story brick row house across the street from the

Mustard Seed Catholic Worker soup kitchen and shelter for the homeless. He rented the top floor to an elderly Black woman, lived on the second floor, and used the first as an art studio.

He had already sacrificed a great deal for peace. He could have rested on his laurels but most certainly did not.

The Eyes, Ears, and Brains of Armageddon

I met Tom Lewis in February of 1981 a week after I left the Capuchin-Franciscan novitiate in Garrison, New York, where I had spent a year preparing to join the order. The friars had recommended me for vows, but I wanted to be more involved in direct service to the poor and peace activism.

My novice master advised me to spend a year doing human service work and then a year at a Catholic Worker community. At the end of that period, he said, if I wanted to return to religious life, I would be more than welcome.

In that first year, I found jobs at a nursing home and group home for mentally challenged adults as well as a volunteer position in a nursery school. I also began attending the weekly Mass at Worcester's Mustard Seed Catholic Worker. One of the community's founders, Michael Boover, whom I had met while getting a degree in religious studies at the College of the Holy Cross in Worcester, introduced me to a Catholic Worker named Margie Farren, who proved to be marvelously friendly.

On our way out from Friday night Mass at the Mustard Seed, Margie pointed to the brick row house across the street and said, "That's Tom Lewis's house. You should meet him. He was one of the Catonsville Nine."

"Oh, wow," I replied, hiding the fact that I had no idea what that was.

Nonetheless, I took up Margie's suggestion and introduced myself to Tom, who turned out to be easy going and not in the slightest bit condescending to a twenty-two-year-old idealist with slender experience in the peace movement.

Tom welcomed me to his house, invited me to dinner, and talked for hours over cold beer and pretzels. I learned that he was a devout Catholic who loved the blues, fishing, and art. He admired masters like Francisco Goya, who depicted the horrors of war. He earned a modest income teaching art at Mark's School, a Southborough prep school and at Worcester Art Museum, but he was no wage slave. He made it clear to all his employers that, from time to time, he might have to, in his words, "risk arrest" over a justice issue.

When I asked what kind of peacework he might be doing, he told me about GTE in Westborough, one of several Massachusetts towns whose suffix often gets shortened to boro, something the natives usually dislike. He told me that site of the multi-billion-dollar corporation had been built to perfect the Command, Control, and

Communications, C³, system for the MX missile, which Tom called "the eyes, ears, and brains of nuclear Armageddon." The missile could carry up to twelve Mark 21 reentry vehicles, each armed with a 300-kiloton W87 warhead.

Tom's apocalyptic description of GTE's program initially struck me as hyperbole but proved accurate.

An MX nuclear missile with components made by GTE for the US military rests on its side in a loading bay.
Salt Lake Tribune *photo*

Founded as General Telephone & Electronics Corporation in 1955, the company qualified as America's largest independent telephone company. Once President Ronald Reagan massively increased military spending, GTE devoted itself to military contracts. By 1981, the company had so little to do with telephones that it legally changed its name to the letters GTE alone, kind of like President Harry S. Truman's middle initial which stood for nothing.

That same year, GTE bought land in Westborough, Massachusetts, and broke ground on a facility designed to create the C³ system for the MX and other nuclear weapons. Tom explained to me that, in the last year of the Jimmy Carter administration, the Pentagon had set aside the nuclear strategy of Mutually Assured Destruction, MAD, and replaced it with a far more dangerous one. Under MAD, the US and Soviet Union deployed land-, air-, and sea-launched nuclear weapons aimed at each other's cities, a policy that had, thus far, dissuaded both superpowers from destroying the planet even though they came very close to doing so during the 1962 Cuban Missile Crisis.

The new policy involved planned deployment of nuclear weapons with Multiple Independent Re-entry Vehicles, MIRV—the Pentagon loves abbreviations—and warheads designed to hit targets with pinpoint accuracy. Under MAD, if the Russians fired at Washington, DC, we fired at Moscow. It made no difference on which particular street warheads landed. Since anti-ballistic defensive weapons had been banned by treaty in 1972, both sides assumed that a nuclear war was suicide. But MIRVs break up after their launch into numerous warheads each targeted on an individual site. They carry a very high explosive yield not vital for attacking cities but essential for destroying hardened targets like missile silos and underground command and control centers.

Designed to hit those very specific targets, MIRVs work essentially as first-strike nuclear weapons. If one side fires its missiles at another, there's no need to destroy empty silos. If, at least theoretically, on the other hand, we can hit our enemy's missiles before they launch, we could confine the destruction to the other country and "win" a nuclear war. The MIRV component discourages opponents from attempting defensive measures. Technology did not and still does not exist to intercept a storm cloud of nuclear weapons.

By deploying the MX on underground constantly moving tracks that burst to the surface only at the moment of launch, the MX missile system also defied any attempt the USSR might make to disarm it on the ground. Typical intercontinental ballistic missiles deploy in stationary silos visible from outer space and inspected by arms control agents. The mobility of the MX created a nuclear whack-a-mole situation. The uncertain location of the MX missiles could provoke the Soviets to obliterate huge rural areas just to be on what they considered the safe side.

Like the sea-launched Trident and air-launched Cruise missiles, the MX was a first-strike nuclear weapon. Novel features of the MX, though unnecessary for Mutually Assured Destruction, were vital for offensive nuclear war.

Unfortunately, what seemed like a stroke of military genius to some proved the opposite. Deploying first-strike nuclear weapons compels our opponents to put their nuclear forces on hair-trigger alert. Any crisis could place the Soviets into a "use them or lose them situation," thus greatly increasing the risk of accidental or intentional nuclear war. Potential deployment of such weapons convinced the *Bulletin of Atomic Scientists* to move its doomsday clock closer to nuclear midnight, the moment of global catastrophe. Ironically, President Reagan called the MX missile, which carried twelve missiles each with thirty times the explosive yield of the Hiroshima Bomb, the Peacekeeper. Deriving its acronym from Missile Experimental, the MX rolled the dice on nuclear annihilation.

Lest readers get so terrified that they decide to put this book aside and watch Netflix, I'm happy to say that those first-strike machinations lost much of their luster in the 1990s when the Pentagon confirmed that even a relatively small nuclear attack could put enough debris in the atmosphere to initiate nuclear winter, a life-extinguishing event caused by the burning effects of nuclear blasts. From the climate-affecting debris sent into the atmosphere by the eruption of Mount Saint Helens in 1980 to the Canadian forest fires in 2023, we know that as few as fifteen nuclear explosions anywhere in the world could blot out the sun everywhere.

Tom spelled out the nuclear nightmare scenario and told me it was being concocted in a brand-new GTE facility twenty-six miles away from Worcester. He then asked if I wanted to join Margie and him in a weekly prayer vigil for disarmament outside the plant. Given my longstanding rhetoric about the urgency of peace activism, how could I refuse?

Inch by Inch

Immediately after reading *A Man for All Seasons*, Thomas Bolt's play about the martyrdom of Saint Thomas More, I wanted to sacrifice my life for my faith. I am not known for patience. If I find something wrong, I want to fix it right away. I assumed heroic people like Tom Lewis were equally compulsive, but that was not true.

Tom believed that, in the face of injustice, he should begin with educating himself, doing considerable prayer, and, if necessary, proceeding to the least confrontational nonviolent act likely to persuade an opponent. He told me if he had a conflict with a neighbor, his first action to resolve things would not be to pour blood on the neighbor's doorstep.

Tom pointed out that the Gospel according to Matthew advises a step-by-step approach to conflict resolution:

> If your brother or sister sins against you, go and tell them their fault, between you and him or her alone. If they listen to you, you have gained your brother or sister. But if they do not listen, take one or two others along with you, that every charge may be established by the evidence of two or three witnesses. If they refuse to listen to them, tell it to the church. And if they refuse to listen even to the church, let them be to you as a Gentile and a tax collector.

Members of the Worcester County Coalition for Disarmament, a secular peace organization founded in 1981, alerted Tom about the GTE contract for the MX. Among those in the coalition: a storyteller named Katie Green; a lawyer named Phil Stone; a Holy Cross grad and former member of the Clamshell Alliance named Matt Shorten; an Assumption College English professor and longtime antiwar activist named Mike True.

On April 25, 1981, the coalition sponsored "An Ecumenical Gathering for Peace" in front of the GTE plant still under construction. Tom joined fifty people at the rain-soaked gathering. He heard Reverend Steven Harvester, a Baptist minister from Worcester, ask God to forgive the US for taking part in the nuclear arms race and Michael True say a civilization that spent so much of its wealth and intelligence on the MX had "collectively lost its marbles." Matt Shorten explained how dangerous first-strike nuclear weapons like the MX were. That concern prompted the coalition to hold several candlelight vigils at GTE.

The groundwork laid by the Worcester County Coalition for Disarmament prompted Tom to become more educated about the MX missile. While doing so, he came to the conclusion that a weekly, nonviolent, spiritually based vigil opposite the new GTE plant's entrance made an appropriate next step.

Despite my time as a friar praying six times a day, I never took to the idea of public prayer, save attending Mass. People who bow their head and say grace before eating make me vaguely uncomfortable. I guess I interpreted Saint Matthew's advice to "pray in secret" as justification for telling people who pray in public, "Get a room."

Tom, on the other hand, began and ended every meal, every meeting, every protest, and every car ride with prayer. He often carried a beat-up paperback Bible with him and offered to share the scriptural readings from the daily Mass. To Tom, the Bible was not a straitjacket or a weapon for browbeating others, but a resource of timeless wisdom. Not a fundamentalist by any means, he did try to take scripture seriously.

He wasn't parochial, either. He had friends who were Buddhist monks, Protestant ministers, and rabbis. He worked with anyone—Black, White, rich, poor, religious, or secular—who cared about peace. He also cited papal and episcopal documents whenever they embraced peace.

Matt Shorten, leader of an interfaith gathering at GTE, says "No to First Strike."
**United Press International photo
front page** *Sunday Telegram* **April 26, 1981**

He reminded me that he had learned a great deal from two holy priests, Dan and Phil Berrigan, to whom he introduced me in time.

He also went to Mass weekly at Saint Joseph's Trappist Abbey in Spencer, where he befriended the abbot and many monks who responded by donating food that Tom took back to the Mustard Seed and poor neighbors. I continue that weekly errand years after Tom's death.

He loved to dig into traditional Catholic feasts and imagery to find a nonviolent core. When he reached a decision to take a certain action, he had satisfied himself that he was not acting on his own ego alone. Despite that, he also insisted that every demonstration be followed by an evaluation to determine how the next one could be closer to the Gospel.

And, so, I started attending the Friday afternoon vigil on the grassy area opposite the sleek silver building filled with more than five hundred high-tech workers who would never see the bloodshed certain to result from their daily efforts. Reaching those well-paid women and men struck me as a formidable challenge.

We drove to Westborough in Tom's old VW bus and brought along many canvas banners saying things like "Use your God-given talents for peace," "No more Hiroshimas, No more Nagasakis, No more MX at GTE." About ten minutes after we arrived on Research Drive, workers drove down GTE's access road and turned left

A vigiler carries the cross at GTE.
photo courtesy of Scott Schaeffer-Duffy

past us on the way to Route 9 toward Boston or Worcester. Some of our banners were colorful and upbeat. Some were dire and bleak. One that we used rarely always seemed to provoke responses. It said, "C^3 is mass Murder."

In general, though, we seldom experienced visible reactions from GTE workers. Good weather was the exception. Holding ten-foot-high banners on poles in a spot exposed to high winds proved arduous. I sometimes felt like one of the soldiers raising the American flag on Iwo Jima. I also had to make my peace with rain, heat, snow, sleet, ice, and boredom.

Time did not exactly fly by. The hour-and-a-half from 3:30 p.m. to 5 p.m. every Friday often seemed much longer. Many weeks, I survived by thinking about the fish and chips dinner that Tom later ordered for all takers from the Pickle Barrel Restaurant down the street from his house. Although I had been a vegetarian for six years, I admit I enjoyed the meal, which reminded me of fish Fridays in my youth before the Second Vatican Council.

Thankfully, Tom, Margie, and I were not the only ones at the vigil. Kate Champa, Ray Demers, Celia Jessa-Ivy, Matt Shorten, Katie Green, Phil Stone, Mike Cahill, Fremont Nantelle, Paul Giaimo, Michael True, Brian Keaney, Chris Douçot, Hazen Ordway, Ray and Lillian Lamothe, Carl Paulson, Dan Lawrence, Dan Ethier, Sue Malone, Ellie Pepper, and others came. Many brought homemade signs. Others took advantage of Tom's considerable collection of banners.

Tom made a few banners with foot-high block letters easily read from the space station. He told me that drivers fifteen feet away can't read a typical two-by-three-foot poster with a message written in black magic marker—not to mention workers looking out wall-to-wall glass windows of the GTE plant a hundred yards up the hill. Too often over the years, I've seen protesters with illegible signs. Not so, Tom's.

One huge disadvantage of standing as we did on public property across the street from the GTE driveway was that we couldn't really chat with the workers. Even passing out leaflets required drivers to roll down their passenger window, lean way over, and stop moving traffic to grab a sheet of paper. The few who paused to say a couple of words earned loud beeping from drivers behind them impatient to get home from work.

In an effort to make a broad religious appeal to GTE employees, we planned a four-day, interfaith event in the grassy area where we vigiled each week. Starting on

Friday, August 6, 1982 at 8:15 a.m., the thirty-seventh anniversary of the US atomic bombing of Hiroshima, and concluding on August 9 at 11:02 a.m., the time when the US bombed Nagasaki, representatives from various faiths prepared prayers for disarmament.

Rabbi Daniel Pernick of Worcester's Temple Emmanuel led a Havdalah service on Saturday just after sundown when the sabbath ended. He told the *Catholic Free Press* reporter, Mary Ellen Murphy, that Protestants, Catholics, and Jews needed to join together to protest the danger of nuclear war.

"In the past," he mused, "if a war was lost, there was still a chance for survival. The consequences of a scenario involving nuclear weapons would be very final."

He explained that the Havdalah is a peaceful service focused on GTE specifically on the horrors of nuclear war. Members of the Temple Emmanuel youth group joined the vigil, according to the rabbi, "because they have chosen nuclear arms as their issue for social action in the upcoming year."

Steven Harvester, a Methodist minister, told a reporter for the *Middlesex News*, "On all our coins, it states that 'in God we trust.' Why is it, then, if there is such a trust, that we must back ourselves up with nuclear weapons?"

Celia Jessa-Ivy told the same reporter, "I like to remember that in every heart there's a human being. I believe that, if we could just get people to open their hearts, they would be able to learn how to live together and not hurt others."

So successful was the event that we repeated it in August of 1990 when folks came from the Noonday Catholic Worker Farm in Winchendon, the Peace Abbey in Sherborn, the Olive Branch community in Worcester, and Sisters from the Little Franciscans of Mary. Reverend Fred Anderson, senior pastor of Worcester's First Baptist Church, offered a prayer. Saffron-robed Nippozan Myohoji Buddhist monks and nuns from the New England Peace Pagoda in Leverett beat drums and chanted in Japanese, "Na mu myoho renge kyo," which, according to the Buddhist website Soka Gakkai, is a

> vow, an expression of determination, to embrace and manifest our Buddha nature. It is a pledge to oneself to never yield to difficulties and to win over one's suffering. At the same time, it is a vow to help others reveal this law in their own lives and achieve happiness.

Father Bernie Gilgun, chaplain of the Mustard Seed Catholic Worker, and Father Leo Barry, pastor of Saint Luke's Church in Westborough, said Mass at the vigil on Sunday morning.

As pastor of a wealthy parish with some members in the arms industry, Father Barry showed courage by standing with us. A year later, during the lead up to the Gulf War, he put a sign in front of Saint Luke's quoting Pope John Paul II: "War in the Persian Gulf would be useless slaughter." Angry parishioners demanded he take the

sign down, so Father Barry said, "Okay" and then put up a different antiwar quote from the pope each week.

The liturgy Father Barry and Father Gilgun offered in August 1990, like most of the prayers, took place under a huge tent we erected in the grass opposite GTE's entrance. The rented tent had fourteen poles and many foot-and-a-half-long metal stakes to secure it from being blown away in the wind. Only in the last hours of the three-day vigil did anyone learn from a Massachusetts Electric employee (their regional office was only a half-mile to our left down Research Drive) that the ground under our tent was riddled with high tension wires that would have electrocuted anyone who struck one. Given how many stakes we used, he told us it was a miracle no one died. The spot sure could have used a dig-safe warning sign.

Sister Clare Carter, Hattie Nestel, and Sandra Lett, from left, top, represent the New England Peace Pagoda as they pray for no more Hiroshimas.
Father Leo Barry and Father Bernie Gilgun say Mass for nuclear disarmament at GTE in August 1990.
photos courtesy of Scott Schaeffer-Duffy

What was the point of all that prayer out of ear shot from GTE workers and pro-nuclear weapons politicians? In 1982, when Mary Ellen Murphy asked Tom Lewis about GTE vigil goals, he said:

We will unite in continual witness, fasting, and prayer that the light of the truth of God's love might penetrate the darkness of this corporation…. With 308 times the explosive force of the Hiroshima bomb, the MX missile represents one of the most dangerous escalations of the arms race. The time is overdue to find new ways of settling conflicts. Our main concern is not active outreach or a publicity drive. The vigil is simply a humble presence held as a reminder of the bombs and a chance to pray that we have learned from history.

Members of Noonday Catholic Worker Farm of Winchendon, Massachusetts, and Worcester's Olive Branch Community vigiled at GTE in August 1990
photo courtesy of Scott Schaeffer-Duffy.

While I imagined a campaign that rushed to carry out civil disobedience so dramatic that it would make national headlines, Tom's deep faith empowered him to treat less flamboyant acts as essential efforts with tremendous potential.

First Civil Disobedience

Almost a year after the first demonstration at GTE, Tom organized an event in which participants would, in his words, "risk arrest." Tom always hoped that any demonstration might bring about a dramatic change of heart in participants, GTE employees, police, judges, politicians, and the public.

Tom felt uncomfortable with protesters who wanted to be arrested and more so with those who wanted to go to jail. He invited others to join months of prayerful meetings to plan an event scheduled for Good Friday, April 9, 1982. Tom, Margie, and Ray Demers reached out to Trappist monks at Saint Joseph's Abbey, who donated a three-foot-high Paschal (Easter), candle for the event. The beautiful candle gave Tom, Margie, and Ray the idea that it could symbolize their desire to bring the light of the resurrection into the darkness of the nuclear arms race.

A couple of weeks before the event, Tom suggested a meeting with Bishop Bernard Flanagan of Worcester. Educated at College of the Holy Cross, also in Worcester, and at the Pontifical North American College in Rome, Flanagan also earned a doctorate in canon law from Catholic University of America in Washington, DC.

Pope John XIII installed Flanagan as bishop of Worcester in 1959. Flanagan attended the Second Vatican Council in Rome from 1962 to 1965 and ardently supported ecumenism. An extraordinary collection of essays entitled, "Blessed Are the Peacemakers: Meditations and Resources on Nuclear Disarmament," published by the diocese Coalition for Justice and Peace, included a 1982 pastoral letter written by Flanagan asserting,

> Presently, the United States and Soviet Russia possess enough nuclear weapons in their arsenals to destroy the world fifteen times over. Does escalation in this situation make any sense?

He went on to urge

> that our government halt all production of nuclear weapons and, to show our good will, to begin a process of nuclear disarmament by a symbolic unilateral act, if necessary, hopefully and ultimately leading to the goal envisioned by the Second Vatican Council of the systemic and total elimination of these destructive weapons.

Two years before the United States Conference of Catholic Bishops issued the 1983 pastoral letter "The Challenge of Peace" where they accepted nuclear deterrence, Flanagan called for unilateral nuclear disarmament.

Despite Flanagan's progressive positions, it seemed kind of old-fashioned to me to seek the bishop's permission for the protest, but Ray told me to relax. He assured me that Tom was not a docile and subservient Catholic.

A meeting in the chancery with Flanagan proved Ray's point. Tom never asked the bishop's permission to commit civil disobedience at GTE on Good Friday. Actually, after describing his vision of the event, Tom invited Bishop Flanagan to join us risking arrest, an invitation the bishop declined. Then Tom asked if the bishop would join a support vigil across the street from GTE, but the bishop more apologetically again said no, so Tom asked, "Will you pray for us on Good Friday?"

Clearly relieved to be offered a low-risk way to support the event, the bishop gladly agreed.

And so, on Good Friday, with what I considered a bit of *chutzpah*, Tom issued a press-release with began,

> Supported by the prayers of our Bishop, along with other Catholic bishops, many of the monks of Saint Joseph's Abbey and communities around the United States, our brothers and sisters outside the gate, and those in similar witnesses today throughout this country, we approach GTE to pray at the risk of arrest in order to bring light to darkness on the afternoon when darkness covered the earth and Christ hung dead on the cross.

Tom had a unique way of using scripture, papal statements, and episcopal writing like Bishop Flanagan's as an opening to draw more clergy and lay Catholics into the circle of activism against nuclear weapons. To me, Tom epitomized the mature rapport between the laity and hierarchy that popes Paul VI and John XXIII envisioned in the Second Vatican Council.

The press release went on to say, "The MX missile represents for us a darkness too great to be ignored. Its enormous cost is a theft from the needy members of our society and the world."

Tom quoted Seattle Archbishop Raymond Hunthausen: "Our nuclear war preparations are the global crucifixion of Jesus," and ended with a citation from the eighteenth chapter of the Gospel according to Saint Matthew: "For where two or three are gathered in my name, I am in the midst of them." He listed the sponsor of the prayer/protest as MX Peace Witness and gave the Mustard Seed Catholic Worker as contact.

The *Catholic Free Press* identified those of us risking arrest as:

Scott Duffy (my pre-marriage last name), 24, of 112 Woodland Street, who works with (mentally-challenged) people; Margaret Farren, 30, of 136 Austin Street, who works with the elderly at a nursing home; Raymond Demers, 34, of 93 Piedmont Street (the Mustard Seed Catholic Worker); Louis (prefers to be called Tom) Doughton, 35, of 29 Merrick Street; Thomas Lewis, 42 of 136 Austin Street, who is an artist and teacher; and Celia Jesa-Ivy, 27, of 28 Crown Street, who is a counselor." All six of us hailed from Worcester's impoverished and ethnically diverse Main South neighborhood.

Tom Doughton told the *Worcester Telegram* that the prayer and protest was not "frivolous" but the culmination of "reflection, fasting, and prayer" that he and others maintained during Lent.

Margie Farren, Scott Duffy, Tom Doughton, Tom Lewis, Celia Jesa-Ivy, and Ray Demers, from left, pray in the GTE driveway as they risk arrest on Good Friday, April 9, 1982

photo by Patrick O'Connor • April, 1982 in *Worcester Magazine*

Celia Jesa-Ivy said she went to GTE because "For a long time, I felt the way to peace is not through weapons. We can't go the weapons route, or ultimately, we will destroy ourselves."

Before our planned civil disobedience, the six of us gathered with forty supporters in our usual vigil spot for a Way of the Cross prayer. Afterwards, we walked slowly across Research Drive. We were met by GTE Security Chief Steven Burns, whom Tom Lewis later called "very nice."

Burns accepted a copy of our statement and a bouquet of flowers.

According to Bennie DiNardo, who reported from the scene for *Worcester Magazine*, Mr. Burns then said, "We fully recognize your right to protest on public property. We ask that you respect our right to private property. May I ask what your intentions are?"

Tom Doughton, who carried the Paschal candle, replied, "We come in prayer" as we processed farther onto GTE property.

Westborough Police Sergeant Richard Brady jumped out of an unmarked car and warned us to leave, or we would be subject to arrest. We knelt and started praying, "Our Father, who art in heaven . . ."

Brady shouted, "I won't have a prayer!"

When we were halfway through our third Hail Mary, three cruisers pulled up. Moments later, officers handcuffed each of us and took us into custody.

Ray Demers later told the *Catholic Free Press*, "We came to pray. We were doing the Spirit's work, not our own, and it had to be carried out. So, we proceeded and were arrested."

Although I had been arrested twice before, I did so with hundreds of people protesting the Trident submarine in Groton, Connecticut. The GTE action was different. My arresting officer at GTE warned me, "You're going to spend the weekend in the Crowbar Hilton," a colorful description of the cells underneath the town's police station.

In Groton, police briefly detained arrestees in a big hall and then released each on personal recognizance until a court date when cases typically continued without a finding or got dismissed. Nobody went to jail in Groton. Some people joked that Groton was "the wading pool of nuclear resistance." An arrest in Westborough promised to be more severe.

After arriving at the Westborough station, police charged us with trespassing and fingerprinted and photographed us. They gave us an opportunity to post fifty dollars bail. Tom Lewis warned us in advance that, if we posted bail, it allowed a judge at trial to fine us that amount, so five of us refused.

Tom Doughton, who had bad experience in police custody for a protest in Spain against the dictator Francisco Franco, paid the bail while the rest of us got taken to five chilly, windowless, basement cells. Each of us found a cell with a filthy, seatless toilet and furnished only with a steel bunk without mattress or blanket. The low ceiling and walls made of riveted steel would have panicked someone with claustrophobia.

While we could not see each other, the open-air bars allowed us to talk, sing, and pray together, activities we did all weekend. On Holy Saturday, a guard brought us coffee, a doughnut, and a copy of the *Worcester Telegram*. I stretched out on my steel bunk and told the others how luxurious I found it to have breakfast, and the paper, served to us in bed. Good acoustics inspired me to dare to sing a rebel tune I learned at Worcester's Tipperary Pub:

> I drink to the death of your manhood,
> those men who'd rather have died
> than to live in the cold chains of bondage
> to bring back their rights were denied.
>
> Where are you now that we need you?
> What burns where the flame used to be?
> Are you gone like the snows of last winter
> and will only our rivers run free?

Years later, I sang the same song on a crowded train in Boston where a rider offered me ten dollars to stop. He never told me what bothered him more, the Irish Republican Army politics or my singing. I must confess, I took the money.

On Easter morning, Father Leo Barry obtained permission to bring us Communion and words of encouragement from Bishop Flanagan. On the back of copies of our leaflet, which the police did not confiscate, I drew sketches and wrote a poem:

Jail Cell
ballpoint pen on paper by Scott Schaeffer-Duffy

Easter 1982

I'm in a jail in Westborough
by Spirit, God, and Son,
with friends and prayers to celebrate
the darkness now is done.

With Tom and Ray and Ceilia,
Myself, and Margie, too,
reborn with Christ inside His tomb,
we leave here to renew

our work for peace, our hopes, and
 prayers,
our lives and loves and dreams.
I can't believe how blessed we are.
Our God is kind, it seems.

They've brought us food from Burger
 King
with bishop's blessings rare
and cherry pies for midnight snacks.
What hotel could compare?

A private bath, a well-lit room
with paper and pen to write,
No window, though our eyes of faith
will see the resurrection light.

My Feet
ballpoint pen on paper by Scott Schaeffer-Duffy

And we will sing and praise him,
this God with Easter spirit.
So full of joy we'll pray, then,
that GTE will hear it.

Tom Lewis later described the weekend in lockup to *Worcester Magazine* as "a positive and reflective experience. We read scriptures, reflected, and prayed together."

Ray Demers told the *Catholic Free Press*, "Being jailed for something you believe in gives you a real sense of freedom and clarity. All of a sudden, the fears that have rendered you helpless before fall into place, making fear unfounded."

The *Free Press* went on to say:

> All the protesters agreed that they were no more saintly or courageous than any other 'baptized Christian,' that they did nothing extraordinary, and that going to jail was in no way to seek martyrdom.

Regarding Tom Doughton accepting bail, Ray said that, outside, Tom "spread the word, connecting those inside the jail with the community" and attended an all-night prayer vigil at Mustard Seed Catholic Worker to emphasize how we considered the GTE witness an opportunity to stand with the poor.

On Monday morning, the police brought us to Westborough District Court where we were arraigned, given a May 11 trial date, and then released.

When we appeared before Judge Francis Larkin, he allowed each of us to make a statement.

"At GTE," said Tom Lewis, "we intended to do God's will and bring light into darkness for those within the plant who accept the madness of the bomb." He went on to quote Bishop Flanagan: "There are times and situations when civil disobedience is not only morally justified but may actually be a duty."

After everyone had spoken, Judge Larkin continued our cases for thirty days without a finding, after which time, if there were no further violations, the charges would be dismissed. He then asked us to each pay twenty-five dollars in court costs.

When we resisted paying any money, the judge asked if we would do community service. I told him that we believed what we did at GTE was community service and that we did not view community service as a punishment.

Tom Lewis then asked if court costs could be given to the poor, an idea that Judge Larkin said he would "look into." The August 11 *Worcester Telegram* headline read, "GTE Protesters to Donate to Poor."

After paying the costs, Tom Lewis told reporters from several newspapers, "Our own feelings are that it was a courageous move on the part of the judge."

When asked why we did not have lawyers, Tom said, "No lawyer can properly represent any action of conscience because the only one who fully understands it is the perpetrator." He concluded by making it clear that, "We cannot rule out civil disobedience or prayer at the risk of arrest as a possibility for future protests."

Even now, so many years later, I can picture Tom's joyful face when he told me he couldn't imagine a better way to spend Easter weekend.

Shareholder Activism

Not satisfied focusing exclusively on GTE at its manufacturing plant in Westborough, opponents of the MX missile also confronted GTE at its corporate headquarters in Stamford, Connecticut, during their 1982 annual meeting of shareholders.

To accomplish the action, eighteen religious communities that each owned GTE stock introduced a resolution for the company to divest itself of military contracts. Specifically, they suggested that GTE

> develop plans for alternative use of MX facilities and plans for alternative employment for displaced workers should the contract be terminated.
>
> The MX plan has from its very inception been a questionable and controversial scheme for protecting land-based ICBMs (inter-continental ballistic missiles) . . .

Furthermore, they adversely affect the domestic economy by generating inflation and by denying workers dignified employment.

Those bringing the resolution to shareholders included the Holy Cross Fathers, Sisters of Charity, Sisters of Notre Dame, Sisters of Saint Joseph, and the Jesuits.

The religious sponsors graciously invited Katie Green, Tom Lewis, Margie Farren, and me to attend the shareholders meeting and speak as their proxies. We drove to the sleek GTE building, visible from I-95 and looking like a rectangular spaceship on a relatively small base. Situated not far from New York City, Stamford was home to many corporations.

The meeting took place in a large hall before an audience of at least five hundred well-dressed, mostly white men.

Two American flags flanked a blue and silver GTE logo hung on a curtained stage behind a long table with more white men, a single woman, and a speaker's podium. On the left, a large screen read LONG RANGE GROWTH. A similar screen on the right projected bar graphs showing $178 million in profit that year.

GTE Shareholders Convene
ink on paper by Scott Schaeffer-Duffy

Prior to consideration of the religious community's proposal, shareholders voted on which of five additional white men should join the board of directors. Speeches lauding GTE's growth as well as consideration of other proposals took precedence, too. I couldn't resist sketching the sole woman on the stage, whose name plate identified her as Dr. Moose. As a Rocky and Bullwinkle fan, I hoped we could count on her vote.

To my surprise, we each had an opportunity to speak. While the others intelligently addressed the potential harm

Dr. Sandra O. Moose, GTE Board Member
ink on paper by Scott Schaeffer-Duffy

of the MX, I chose to introduce myself as a descendant on my mother's side of two passengers on the *Mayflower* as well as two signatories of the Declaration of Independence. Figuring shareholders might consider disarmament an anti-American plot by communist sympathizers, I stressed that I had learned as a Boy Scout that our nation differed from those that threaten global peace and security. I appealed to them to support the religious proposal as a patriotic gesture as well as a moral and intelligent one.

Thankfully, many shareholders voted to disarm GTE. Unfortunately, they represented only two percent of the total vote. Nonetheless, impressing me with their persistent efforts to convince GTE to drop a $375 million dollar contract for the MX missile, the Worcester County Coalition for Disarmament continued to support similar resolutions by religious communities at the next six shareholder meetings.

A Stronger Approach

In August 1982, I joined Saint Benedict's Catholic Worker in Washington, DC, but kept in touch with Tom about efforts to disarm GTE. The monks at Saint Joseph Abbey in Spencer, Massachusetts, loaned Margie Farren a loom and hired her as well as Carol Markarian, a woman Katie Green described as "committed to a life of simplicity and meditation," to weave liturgical stoles and other items for the Holy Rood Guild.

Carol, a deeply contemplative religious person, joined the vigil at GTE. In early December, Tom invited me to risk arrest again at GTE with Father Jim Connolly, pastor of Saint Blaise Church in Bellingham, Massachusetts; Theresa Guisti from the Mustard Seed Catholic Worker; Margie, Carol, and himself. By that time, I had fallen in love with a Catholic Worker named Claire Schaeffer, whom I would marry in 1984. She

Gazette Photo by BOB MORIN

MX Peace Witness members stand at Westboro District Court after their arraignment this morning. They are, from left, Carol Markarian, Margaret Farren, Scott Duffy, the Rev. James Connolly, Tom Lewis and Theresa Guisti.

and I took a bus to Worcester and learned details of the protest Tom planned to lead on December 28, the Feast of the Holy Innocents, a day when Catholics recall how King Herod slaughtered all of Bethlehem's infants in hopes of killing the newborn King of the Jews.

Unlike the first civil disobedience, we planned to carry more than a candle and flowers ten feet onto GTE property. This time, early in the morning when workers had just begun to arrive, we'd be dropped off at the front and rear entrances to the GTE plant where we would pour blood in the shape of a cross on the concrete and then kneel in prayer for disarmament. To accomplish the plan, a student from UMass Medical School drew blood from each of us, put it into baby bottles, and stored it in Tom's fridge.

Claire planned to join the regular legal vigil that afternoon. If security and the police processed us in time and released us on personal recognizance, the six of us would all join her there.

To tell you the truth, I had quite a bit of trepidation about the action. I thought GTE workers would be enraged when they had to step over bloody crosses to get to their jobs. In the end, though, I trusted Tom's activist experience and the prayerfulness of the entire group.

Like Tom Lewis and Margie Ferron, Scott Schaeffer Duffy kneels in prayer in the GTE yard in August 1982.
photo by Rick Sennott
August, 1982 in *Middlesex News*

After Father Jim, Carol, and Theresa got dropped at the front door, Tom, Margie, and I got out at the back. We crossed a pedestrian bridge and poured blood on the cement to make three eight-foot-long crosses. It had rained the night before, leaving the ground so wet that the blood spread out in a dramatic fashion. While GTE public affairs manager Claire Deveney would later tell the *Boston Globe* she believed the "red liquid substance" we used may have been "ketchup," I don't think anyone who saw the crosses doubted we had used anything other than real human blood.

Along with Tom and Margie, I knelt and waited for the hammer to fall. To my surprise, most of the workers passed us in silence while several apologized for working on the MX. One woman asked us to pray for her. No one chastised us. It felt as if the employees recognized bloodshed as the inevitable consequence of working for GTE. Many workers took copies of our statement which said:

We come in the spirit of humility and love for our brothers and sisters at GTE. We pour our own blood in the sign of the cross as a sobering sign of first-strike death. … We are here today to announce the good news that life is sacred and that we cannot stand by in silence while the slaughter of the human community is being planned in our own backyard.

Not notified in advance of our action, Westborough police arrived in fifteen minutes and placed us under arrest. As fortune would have it after processing us, the police brought us to Westborough District Court where we were arraigned and released in time to join the vigil. When I arrived, someone asked me to describe what we had done. I demonstrated by kneeling down, hat in my hand, and bowing my head. Unbeknown to me, Rick Sennott from the *Middlesex News*, took a picture of me. The Associated Press acquired the photo, which ran the next day in the *New York Daily News* with the caption:

PROTEST PRAYER—Scott Duffy, a member of the Catholic Worker Movement from Washington, DC, prays outside the Westboro, Massachusetts, offices of GTE Corp's Strategic Systems Division plant Tuesday after a protest against work being done for the MX missile.

The Boston Globe ran a large photo of Claire and me arm in arm beside a banner reading "Pray for Disarmament." In a *Middlesex News* article entitled "6 spill blood in Westboro MX protest," Theresa Guisti was quoted as saying, "I believe the doing of justice is an extension of the works of mercy." Even the *New York Times* covered the protest.

To his credit, while he often reached out to the press, Tom stressed that the internal integrity of each action mattered more than publicity. He told me that a sacrificial act for peace could have an immeasurable mystical significance even if no one knew about it.

Tom's dear friend Phil Berrigan went further, calling the press "The Gong Show."

Michael True later advised me, "When talking to a reporter, keep your statement short, speak slowly, repeat it two or three times, ask the reporter to read it back to you, and then brace yourself for the unrecognizable version that makes its way into print." Since Claire has often reported for the *National Catholic Reporter*, I admit that some reporters do the job more professionally.

On January 27, 1983, one month after our arrest, we appeared for trial before Judge William F. Brewin in Westborough District Court. Brewin cut off any attempt to explain why we opposed the MX. He told us he would not allow political statements in his courtroom. Brewin even threatened Tom Lewis with contempt when he tried repeatedly to quote Bishop Flanagan.

Father Connolly later told the *Catholic Free Press*, "The spirit of the American judicial system was lost in the trial."

"It was courtroom street fighting," Michael True said. "The judge would not let the defendants make any moral or political statements, yet he did not hesitate to voice his sentiments on actions of civil disobedience and the presence of the MX missile in our society."

With the proceedings reduced to "Were we on GTE property?" and "Did we refuse to leave when asked to do so?" a conviction for trespass proved inevitable.

After announcing guilty verdicts for all six of us, Judge Brewin cited Tom's arrest record as justification for giving him thirty days in jail, the maximum sentence.

After Carol said, "I can't morally pay (fifty-dollar) court costs because I don't feel what I did was an injustice. I am doing justice by making the world aware that it will be destroyed by nuclear war," the judge gave her ten days in jail.

Margie, Theresa, and I each got thirty days with twenty suspended on probation.

Father Connolly was put on probation and charged fifty dollars in court costs. The judge told him, "If the Moonies (members of the Unification Church) protested the practice of the Catholic Church on your parish's property, you'd be the first one in court."

At the conclusion of sentencing, Brewin told all the defendants, "Some of us aren't opposed to the MX missile if it is important for the defense of the country. I respect your right to protest, but only within the framework of the law."

The *Evening Gazette* reported that one of the protesters then yelled at Judge Brewin, "You are complicit in preparing the world for nuclear holocaust." Frankly, I don't recall that at all.

As court officers escorted us downstairs to probation, friends and supporters, who packed the courtroom, began singing, "Were you there when they crucified my Lord?"

"That's a bit overblown, don't you think?" Tom quipped.

Minutes later, Father Connolly was released, and the probation officer gave Theresa, Margie, Carol, and me forms to sign. After seeing that they included a promise to obey the law while on probation, we declared we could not promise that. The exasperated officer brought us back into the empty courtroom where the then furious judge said he would see us again after ten days in jail when, if we still refused to sign, we'd get the full thirty days.

Later that afternoon, Tom and I arrived by police transport at Worcester County Jail. Following Tom's advice, I kept quiet and observed the scene rather than blabbing about why we were in jail. In a drab, windowless room, a guard ordered each of us to strip and put all our possessions in plastic bags. After standing naked for a bit, we each received a pair of boxers, blue jeans, a white tee-shirt, a button denim shirt, a set of sheets, a wool blanket, a towel, a bar of soap, a cheap toothbrush, and a minuscule tube of generic toothpaste. Many of the clothes felt cold and damp. To my surprise, I was allowed to keep my breviary, a book of prayers recited throughout the day, and the guards permitted Tom to keep his Bible.

Guards marched us down a hall along with about six other prisoners not associated with the GTE action and past a row of cubicles with telephones facing plexiglass windows with similar phones on the other side where prisoners sat for non-contact visits. We came to the entrance of the maximum-security cell blocks, but to our surprise, turned down another hall to the jail infirmary where a room typically used for sick inmates had been converted into an extension of maximum security because of overcrowding.

Although we were convicted only of a misdemeanor, every new inmate at Worcester County went to maximum security until they could be classified about a week later. Our quarters consisted of a reasonably bright and tidy white room with sixteen bunk beds, a television set, and an adjacent bathroom with two showers. A small table with four chairs sat in a corner, affording the men somewhere to play cards or other games.

A sizable desk sat on the side where a guard kept watch. He was responsible for counting us four times a day and leading the way to the steel-tabled cafeteria for meals.

The average age of the inmates couldn't have been higher than twenty-two. They were sometimes coarse but no more so than many of my own friends. Mostly, they focused on their own issues and on the desire to get out of jail as soon as possible. They somehow ascertained why we were in jail and thereafter called Tom "Proton" and me "Neutron," pretty clever nicknames in my opinion.

During my first time in county jail, I marveled at how inmates didn't match stereotypes I'd gleaned from movies. Sure, some of the guys lifted weights whenever they had the opportunity to do so, but, on the whole, the atmosphere wasn't oppressively macho. Being in pretty much the same boat spurred people to tread lightly on each other's feet. I liked some of the men very much and didn't really dislike anybody.

On our second night, a young guard stormed in at 10 p.m., slamming his attendance book on the desk before yelling, "Turn off the goddamned TV and get in your bunks right now! Lights out!"

All the other guards let us watch TV with the volume down low until midnight. Smelling the aroma of alcohol on the guard's breath, Tom figured the fellow had been called into work from a party or bar and was taking his anger out on us.

In any event, the men begrudgingly followed his orders. A few minutes later, though, one of the guys started fake snoring like Curly used to do on *The Three Stooges*. Although very quiet, it prompted another man to start snoring like Shemp with a long build-up and staccato follow-through. Others joined in.

The guard finally shouted, "All right, cut the shit! Anyone making more noise is going to lockup!"

His threat settled things down but only for a couple of minutes before an inmate started to hum "The Star-Spangled Banner." Others joined in to raise the volume. Finally, everyone, including Tom and I, hummed with gusto, reminding me powerfully of the scene in *Animal House* when the frat boys sing the National Anthem to thwart

Dean Wormer from expelling them. I doubted the guard could justify sending thirty-two men to lockup for patriotic fervor.

Finally, the beleaguered corrections officer shouted, "You can all go to Hell!" and stormed out of the infirmary.

Not long afterwards, someone calmly got out of bed and turned the TV back on. A few others settled into chairs to watch with him. I felt like I had just witnessed something more akin to the movie *Gandhi* than *Shawshank Redemption*.

Then, to my surprise, the next morning, to alleviate overcrowding, the jail administrators furloughed a few others and me convicted of nonviolent crimes. Because of that, I appeared before Judge Brewin on February 6 through the front door rather than from one of the basement cells like Theresa and Margie. Having completed her ten-day sentence by then, Carol had already been released.

Eventually, Theresa, Margie, and I sat together in the front row of the courtroom while the judge heard other matters. All the while, Theresa sat upright with her eyes closed and hands resting calmly in her lap. When we were finally called, Judge Brewin asked us if a taste of jail had convinced us to agree to sign the probation forms.

Margie said, because Saint Joseph's Abbey needed her to begin a project right away, she would sign.

I told the judge, "I don't intend to disobey the law, but I can't promise I won't some time. I don't want to be double bound by the court as well as by my conscience."

When called on, Theresa opened her eyes and said, "Your honor, we made our position clear at trial. If you have nothing different to say now, please send me back to jail right away, or I'll miss gym."

Needless to say, Judge Brewin was unimpressed, so Theresa and I got sent back to jail to complete the thirty-day sentences.

Thankfully, Worcester County returned me to the infirmary with Tom. Over the next days, I befriended a middle-aged, illiterate guy. He asked if I would read him letters from his wife and pen replies that he'd dictate.

I agreed and soon discovered that the guy had been sentenced to six months for driving without a license, something he couldn't get because he couldn't read. Despite the lack of a license, he continued driving for work to support his wife and three small kids.

In her letters, his wife unsuccessfully tried to convey that everything was okay at home with her and the children. I could feel the man's anguish that he couldn't support them. His guilt-laden letters gushed with love for her and the children.

Being an intermediary between them broke my heart and angered me at the justice system that couldn't help the family instead of tearing it apart. On visiting day, when Claire came to visit me, I saw him pressing his hands against the glass partition to match the palms of his children and wife on the other side. In a world where suffering from natural disasters and disease already causes so much pain, does it serve any meaningful purpose to add needless suffering?

The time in jail, like my work sheltering the homeless, underscored for me the evil of spending hundreds of millions of dollars on suicidal weapons when so many human needs went and go unmet.

While Tom and I were incarcerated, a letter by Michael True appeared in the *Worcester Telegram* saying:

> Because Judge Brewin sent five of my friends to jail, there are fewer people feeding the hungry and housing the homeless at Catholic Worker houses in Worcester and Washington, DC. I think GTE strongly resembles Krupp, the manufacturer of armaments in Hitler's Germany. I think GTE ought to be stopped.

Tough words.

The Walls of Jericho and More

While the weekly vigil continued, Tom Lewis, Katie Green, and members of the Mustard Seed organized a biblical protest for Good Friday, which happened to be on April Fool's Day in 1983.

Inspired by Israelites beating drums and blowing horns while marching round the fortified city of Jericho, a tactic that miraculously made the walls come tumbling down,

Anti-Bomb Protesters Picket at Westboro GTE Plant

WESTBORO — Protesters from the Mustard Seed, the Worcester Catholic Worker house, marched in front of the GTE building off Route 9 yesterday afternoon. One demonstrator, Thomas Lewis, said the theme of this Good Friday protest was "The Walls of Jericho." The anti-bomb protesters hope to bring attention to the plant where research for the guidance systems for the MX missile is being done.

sixty people marched back and forth in front of GTE with large banners, a wooden drum, and a trumpet. Many in the procession wore dramatic gray cloaks, carried blood red banners on tall poles, and followed a person carrying a large wooden cross. Save the sound of the instruments, the marchers were silent. Afterwards, Sister Annette Rafferty led the group in prayer.

Four Westborough police officers and GTE security personnel on hand did not intervene, since all the protesters stayed outside the guardrails nearby and not on GTE property. Having returned to the Catholic Worker in DC, I did not attend the event but heard from many who did that it resonated strikingly.

Two months later, on Sunday, June 19, thirty peace groups and religious

On April 1, 1982, flag-waving marchers emulate Israelites bringing down the biblical walls of Jericho.
April, 1982 in *Middlesex News*

"Max, we can't arrest all these people. What the hell are we going to do?"

April, 1982 in *Peacework*

organizations along with the Worcester County Coalition for Disarmament, co-sponsored a large demonstration at GTE. Called Building a Peaceful Future, the event featured a diverse group of speakers, including Margaret Burnham, director of the National Conference of Black Lawyers; Carol Doherty, president of the Massachusetts Teacher's Association; Tess Ewing, president of Boston School Bus Drivers; Allen Key, president of Business Alert to Nuclear War; Jessica Shubow of Boston Women's Pentagon Action; Leslie Cagan of Mobilization for Survival; and Kip Tiernan of Poor People's United Fund.

Three musicians, two mimes, and a sign-language interpreter joined the program. A letter from Worcester County Coalition for Disarmament called on moral, technical, political, and social grounds for an end to GTE's work on the MX. Reva Beck, spokesperson for the coalition, told the *Evening Gazette* that the event, one of 150 similar protests taking place around the world on that date, was crucial to demonstrate opposition to continued nuclear weapons buildup.

The following morning, a hundred protesters who had all taken part in nonviolence training crossed Research Drive and sat down in GTE's driveway. The total blockade prompted a dozen Westborough police officers at the scene to work in pairs to carry demonstrators off the road and GTE property. Although participants had prepared for legal consequences, the police—perhaps because of the large numbers—didn't arrest anyone.

Interestingly, a few demonstrators some thirty-odd years later received much harsher penalties than the blockaders at GTE. On October 22, 2020, Lauren Handy, 28, of Alexandria, Virginia; John Hinshaw, 67, of Levittown, New York; Heather Idoni, 61, of Linden, Michigan; William Goodman, 52, of the Bronx; and Herb Geraghty, 25, of Pittsburgh blocked the entrance to a Washington, DC abortion clinic using their bodies, furniture, chains, and ropes.

The activists live-streamed their protest on Facebook. They were held in prison until trial. On August 29, 2023, a jury found them guilty of a Freedom of Access to Clinic Entrances Act offense and felony conspiracy against rights. The defendants each faced up to a maximum penalty of eleven years in prison, three years of supervised release and fines up to $350,000. They were returned to prison until sentencing. They all received long jail sentences. Lauren Handy was sentenced to four years and nine months. On January 23, 2025, President Trump pardoned Handy and her eight co-defendants.

In my forty-five years of peace activism, I have participated in many blockades of weapons plants, military bases, and the Pentagon. In some instances, the blockade closed the facilities for hours and once for an entire day, but I never faced such draconian legal consequences.

On July 21, 1983, though, Kathryn A. Lee, a reporter for the *Worcester Telegram* wrote an article entitled Protest at GTE Draws Mixed Reaction. Five Westborough residents weighed in. Robert J. Dean said, "I don't particularly object to what they're doing, as long as it's peaceful."

Anthony J. Pieroni had a gloomy take: "There's no hope. It's a good effort, but there's no avoiding God's plan. What's going to happen is going to happen—nuclear holocaust, God's Second Coming."

Cindy L. Dayotas had mixed views: "We should be as strong as the Russians, but I hope it doesn't come to nuclear war. I think (the rally at GTE) will make a difference. It brings public awareness, and because of that, you have to do something."

Diane M. Gentilotti went whole hog in favor of the protests: "It's the only way you get heard. Those who sit back and don't do anything never get anywhere."

The last person interviewed, Elaine L. Lyons, was equally emphatic: "I don't want nuclear weapons. I don't want anything to do with wars. And sometimes the smallest group can make the biggest noise."

Peace Pentecost, 1983

After my release from Worcester County Jail for my part in pouring blood at GTE, I returned to Saint Benedict's Catholic Worker where Claire and I worked part-time as receptionists for *Sojourners Magazine*, published by antiwar evangelical Christians who lived in a community called Sojourners. We learned about many nonviolent campaigns. One in particular caught our attention: Peace Pentecost 1983. On May 22 that year, the day Christians celebrate God's gift of the Holy Spirit, Sojourners offered prayer, speakers, and music at the National Cathedral, followed the next day by civil disobedience in the Rotunda of the US Capitol to protest a bill funding the MX missile. The event was one of many national efforts to scrap the MX and coincided with the campaign at GTE in Westborough.

Claire and I along with our dear friend Carl Siciliano, who had joined Saint Benedict's months earlier, attended the Sunday evening prayer service at the enormous National Cathedral in Northeast DC. Music and speakers uplifted the crowd of several thousand filling the pews. While Claire held down the Dorothy Day Catholic Worker fort on Monday, Carl and I joined about five hundred others sitting and kneeling in the rotunda while Father Richard Rohr stood in the center in his Franciscan habit to lead prayers for the end of funding the MX missile.

In comparison to the violent invasion of the Capitol thirty years later by an angry mob trying to overturn the election of Joe Biden, the prayer and subsequent arrest took place without any injury or ill feeling. Gradually, Capitol police escorted us to buses that transported us to DC Central Cellblock where we spent the night crowded in large holding cells.

The next day at arraignment, most people paid a fine to close the matter, but a dozen of us asked for a trial, among them Father Tom Lumpkin of the Detroit Catholic Worker along with Carl and me. At the conclusion of our trial, the prosecutor recommended thirty days in jail, but the judge exclaimed, "Haven't you been listening to these people at all?" He sentenced us to three days after making sure that Monday would count as a full day even though we wouldn't get into the jail until night, and that we'd be released early in the morning on the third day. He essentially sentenced us to about thirty-eight hours, the shortest jail sentence I've ever had.

True to the judge's words, the DC jail spit Carl and me out at 7 a.m. into a courtyard where a massive steel gate opened before us. Each of us wearing a t-shirt embossed with the word JAIL, I walked out while Carl danced to the street shouting, "Free at last! Free at last!"

An elderly man, walking by with his wife, said to her, "They must have been in there a long time!"

A year later, Claire and I married and moved to Worcester, Massachusetts, where we rejoined the weekly vigil at GTE. Oftentimes, only a handful of people held banners and signs each Friday, but our experience in DC reminded us that opposition to the MX stretched far beyond Westborough. Our efforts, small as they might be, joined those of others around the nation.

Good Friday, 1984

In a year when many believed George Orwell had accurately predicted the future, Tom gathered a new group to prayerfully plan another act of civil disobedience at GTE. Would-be civil disobedients included Sue Malone, a Westborough resident, registered nurse, mother of four, and organist at Saint Luke's Church; Michael True, professor of American literature at Assumption College and father of six; Mary Laurel True, a bilingual social worker with the elderly and Michael's daughter; Dan Lawrence, a carpenter and former Trappist monk; Tom Lewis, Claire Schaeffer whom I married in June, and me.

Our statement still moves me.

Sue Malone, front, and Michael True, Mary Laurel True, Tom Lewis, Claire Schaeffer, Scott Duffy, and Dan Lawrence, from left, pray on Good Friday, 1984, in GTE's driveway.
April, 1984 in *Worcester Patch*

We come to GTE to pray and reflect with you as workers. We come to reflect on our common fate that a nuclear death is never more than six minutes away and the terrifying reality that, for the first time in history, the future is no longer a certainty but an option.

We come to reflect on the Love of God, a wondrous creative Love which not only brought all life into being but also, in spite of the Bomb, has miraculously sustained us this long. We come this Good Friday especially to reflect on a divine Love so profound that it was carried even unto death, death on a Cross.

We come in a spirit of Penance to ask forgiveness

for our complicity in the arms race, for our taxes which pay for weapons, for our failure to protest enough on behalf of life, for the violence in our hearts, for our leaders who propose war-making, and for those who help construct the weapons themselves. For these things we are sorry.

And yet we come simultaneously in Hope to recall that a nuclear crucifixion is not the final word, but that God's Love triumphs even over death. As Father Daniel Berrigan of the Society of Jesus says, "Though the Bomb speaks loud, it cannot speak last." Our personal experience teaches us to hope in a Love of God which reaches beyond all barriers and empowers us to envision a world without the Bomb. Scripture tells us that neither principalities nor powers, courts nor jails, torture nor death can deter this Hope.

We come with wonder at the God-given Peace which begins by our joining together in prayer, a Peace the Bomb never gives. "We need prayer," said Dorothy Day, "for strength to know and to love and to find out what to do and set our hand to useful work that will contribute to peace, not to war.

May that Prayerful Peace grow until it overcomes all thought and deeds of war-making. Amen

On March 22, members of our group, calling ourselves Peace Witness at GTE, sent a letter to the plant's public relations director inviting workers to pray with us on Good Friday.

While twenty supporters from around the area held a sign reading, "GTE Workers, meet us to Pray for Peace," my then fiancée, Claire Schaeffer, told the *Middlesex News*, "I know we are taking a big risk by coming to pray with a chance of being arrested, but we hope our risk will inspire GTE workers to take a small risk."

Unfortunately, when with Bibles, prayer books, and flowers in hand we crossed Research Drive into GTE's driveway on Good Friday, April 20, 1984, the only people we met were Westborough police and plant security. Following three warnings, the seven of us were arrested for trespassing and disorderly conduct.

Regarding the religious nature of the protest, Tom Lewis later told *Worcester Magazine*:

Religion has always been a focus of my life. You need the strength that is to be gained from prayer and reflection, and some kind of value system that will give meaning to your life. In the sixties, we (religious activists) were not accepted by the peace movement. We were out of the mainstream, but in the seventies, peace activism literally stopped all over, with the exception of those of us with a religious base. I just say that as a reality. It's not an indictment of anybody. All that's changed is that spiritually based protest has become more visible. One of the reasons it has become more visible is that other things have stopped.

"The times require this type of involvement. Organized religion is being challenged," said Rabbi Stanley David.

Reverend Paul Ferrin added,

> Fear often brings people back to organized faith. The threat and the hope have brought people back to religion—the threat that the world is going to actually have an Armageddon, and the hope that religion has a vision for worldwide peace. The stakes are too large for the churches not to get involved."

Sister Annette Rafferty of the Sisters of Saint Joseph weighed in:

> I am involved out of conviction that there is a connection between women's struggles, militarism, violence against women, and violence by a government that cuts child nutrition in favor of building the MX missile.

Bill Penney, a researcher at the University of Massachusetts Medical Center who attended the support vigil, told the *Worcester Telegram*, "We want to let others know that we care about the world we live in."

The *Middlesex News* quoted me as saying,

> I'd be happier if GTE allowed us to pray. I'd also be happier if police didn't arrest us when the only crime here is the arms race. I'd be happier if they had arrested the GTE executives.

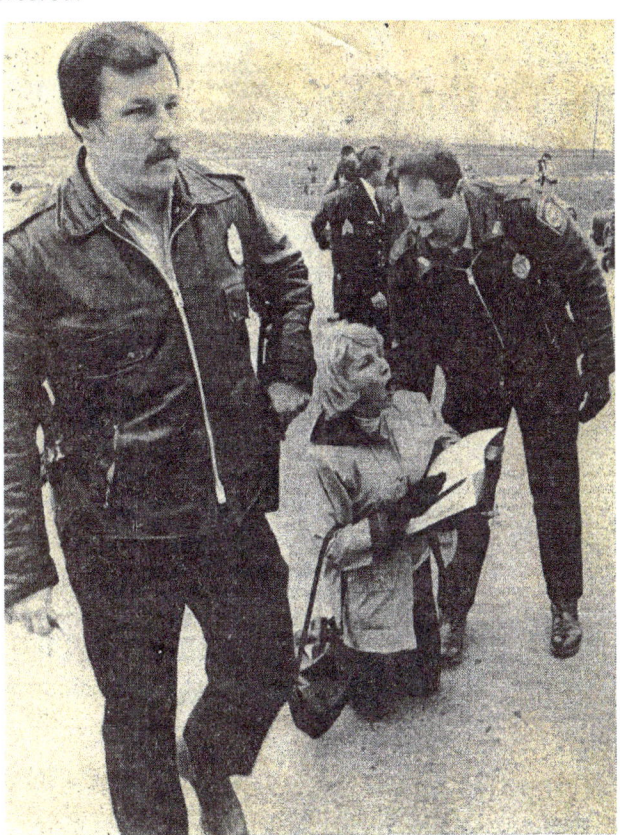

Westborough Police arrest Sue Malone at GTE on Good Friday, 1984, as she prays for an end to weapons design and manufacture of weapons components at the plant.
April 21, 1984 in *Worcester Telegram*

Dan Lawrence told the *Daily Item*,

> The goal of the prayer vigil was that, through prayer, GTE would terminate their work on development of the C^3 trigger systems for the MX missile. We regard prayer as a powerful means to peace.

After her arrest, Sue Malone summed up her rationale, in the *Catholic Free Press* for joining the prayer/protest:

> I did this to a make a personal statement because I had reached a level of frustration working within the legal realm. It just was not enough. It was not until middle America stood up that anything happened to stop the Vietnam War. I am middle America. I am

7 arrested at GTE plant

Police arrest Claire Schaeffer, left, and Michael True at GTE on Good Friday, 1984.
April 21, 1984 in *Middlesex News*

a church organist, and my husband is a college professor and a school committeeman. I was hoping to shake people up a little and make them see that the Boy Scouts and PTA mean nothing if the world blows up.

She also said the risk of jail was "a small price to pay if people open their eyes and see what is going on."

Trial was set for May 30 in Westborough District Court. We sent out formal invitations to people who might attend, as if GTE were on trial rather than us.

On May 24, Claire wrote the following letter to Archbishop Bernard Law in Boston:

Dear Archbishop Law,

It is with great joy that I read in Monday's *Boston Globe* of the Easter Peace witness at Avco (a subsidiary of Textron which manufactured MX and Pershing II missiles in Wilmington, Massachusetts). What better way to celebrate the reality of the Resurrection than to take that reality into a place where Death seems to be so prevalent.

I was deeply moved, in particular, by the presence of Father Bob Branconnier, who lifted up the Body of Christ inside the grounds of Avco.

To me, a lay Catholic, his actions embodied hope and gave me direction for the course of my resistance to the development of nuclear weapons. We must take the Crucifixion and Resurrection of our Lord Jesus into the death factories; these Truths will lay the ground for conversion.

I am pleased to see that a priest and lay people are taking (Worcester) Bishop Bernard Flanagan's words on the need for civil disobedience (perhaps it is more appropriate to say Divine Obedience):

But as the hands of the nuclear clock move closer to midnight, is the God of peace calling more believers to also consider non-violent civil disobedience as a faithful response to the crisis? Many of us are understandably afraid of breaking the law and the consequences, but "Love casts out fear," and divine light and strength will be with us, if we ask for them in prayer and community.

What greater prayer and community is there than the Eucharist? I thank God that Christ rose at Avco this Easter.

On Good Friday, seven of us from Worcester, Clinton, and Westborough took prayer onto the property of GTE. Our hope was to pray with GTE employees as a first step towards making peace. I enclose our two invitations to prayer as well as an article describing the witness.

It is my hope that more such witnesses as the recent ones at Avco and GTE will occur again and again. We need such a presence in Massachusetts. This state is slated to receive the third largest amount of funding for MX development; only California and Colorado exceed us. According to John Feahy of Avco Systems Division in Burlington, "Approximately fifty percent of our (Avco's) business is related to the MX." In the midst of so much darkness, we need all the light we can get.

You, who hold the Paschal Candle in the Church, please bless and pray for those who hold up the same light in the midst of the darkness of nuclearism.

On the following day, May 25, Roland G. Werme had an equally forceful letter in the *Catholic Free Press*:

Dan Lawrence, left, and Tom Lewis arrive at court to be arraigned as a result of the Good Friday, 1984 presence at GTE.
April 1984 in *Worcester Magazine*

I wonder if the GTE workers know that after the defeat of Hitler's Germany in World War II, in which Europe was left in ruins and thirty million people had been killed, devout Catholics and pious Protestants in Germany, after viewing Auschwitz and the other death camps, said, "I was only a clerk in the registration office"; "I thought there were cattle in those boxcars on the railroad"; "I was only doing my duty as a loyal German"; "I had to be a party member in order to hold my job"; "I was only carrying out orders from above"; "I did not know what was going on"; "I was told I must do my part to save the world from Communism."

He went on to challenge the GTE workers to wrestle with their consciences by remembering "the Westborough Seven and what they stand for and will stand up for in the Westborough District Court." He urged "all concerned citizens" to come to the trial.

After reading that letter, I thought, "Sue Malone really did shake people up."

In preparation for the May 30 trial, I recalled Abraham Lincoln's observation, "The man who represents himself has a fool for a client." While I didn't want to lose the opportunity to speak on my own behalf, I didn't enjoy being told that what I really wanted to say was irrelevant. Having participated in a model United Nations as a high school student, I understood that most institutions had procedural rules to maintain order.

While many of our supporters characterized Judge Brewin's restrictions on our testimony in our previous trial as unjust, one could also say that we had not established the relevance of introducing the rationale for civil disobedience. Once one understands Robert's *Rules of Order*, for example, one can see how the protocols actually protect individual rights to be heard, unlike mob rule with every person trying to shout down the other.

After learning that some anti-nuclear activists had used a defense called "necessity" to make their motives relevant, I thought we might try it. In a nutshell, the necessity defense argues that an individual can be justified breaking a law in order to prevent greater harm. The classic example is entering a burning building to save lives. The usual authority of no-trespassing signs takes a back seat in an emergency. If the harm is great enough, action to prevent that harm can be not only justifiable, but necessary.

However, it is important to stress that necessity does not justify all lawbreaking. To prevent overwhelming courts with frivolous arguments for breaking laws, a legitimate defense of necessity has requirements. In the case of *Commonwealth vs. Paul Hood*, a military veteran, peace activist, and friend, Massachusetts justices ruled that necessity should be upheld only when

1) the defendant is faced with a clear and imminent danger, not one that is speculative

2) the defendant can reasonably expect his/her action will be effective as the direct cause of abating the danger

3) there is no legal alternative which will be effective in abating the danger

4) the legislature has not acted to preclude the defense by a clear and deliberate choice regarding the values at issue

Breaking into a burning building to save lives is not necessary if the fire is imaginary, if firefighters are nearby, or if someone tries to extinguish the blaze with gasoline or another means unable to stop it.

I read the Hood decision in the law library of Worcester Superior Court and spent many hours following the trail of cases cited. Through that tedious, pre-internet method, I became familiar with numerous other necessity cases. Armed with that knowledge and the permission of my co-defendants, I wrote a motion for the right to use a necessity defense. The opening and closing paragraphs of the three-page brief:

> Your honor, the availability of this defense, and our constitutional right to present the evidence to support it are guaranteed by principles established in *United States vs. May* (622 Fed. Reporter, 2d 1000-1010), *Commonwealth vs. Averill* (423 N.E. 2nd 6-8), *Commonwealth vs. Brugmann* (433 N.E. 2nd 1109), Commonwealth *vs. Hood* (452 N.E. 2d 188-198), *State vs. Marley* (509 P.R. 2d 1109), and most especially under the Pennsylvania Superior Court decision rendered on February 17, 1984 of *Commonwealth vs. Berrigan*.
>
> Given our offer to introduce evidence to meet conditions set under Massachusetts law, the availability of the necessity defense is a legal right. To deny that right is to impose a gag rule, reducing this trial to testimony to the fact of simple trespass, facts we do not contest. The difference between ours and a case of simple trespass lies clearly in the special circumstances of the imminent threat of nuclear war, GTE's contribution to that threat, the lack of effective legal means to address it, and our reasonable belief that prayer with GTE workers for peace is effective. To disallow evidence to support a necessity defense in our circumstance suggests a naive appraisal of the nuclear threat, a disrespect for our right to believe in the efficacy of prayer, and a denial of our legal rights. It also affords a complete legal cover for the supremely dangerous nuclear first-strike work being done at GTE.
>
> We sincerely hope the court will not afford that cover, but let this issue be dealt with on its merits in open court.

After Judge Philip Tracy ruled that we could claim necessity, we structured our defense around proving that we had met conditions for necessity at GTE. In support of the imminent threat of nuclear war posed by first-strike weapons at GTE, Claire introduced evidence from The Union of Concerned Scientists, Sue questioned Dr. Tom Winters from Physicians for Social Responsibility, and I raised concerns from the organization High Tech Professional for Peace.

We closely questioned Steven Burns, the GTE security manager, on the plant's nuclear weapons work. On the ineffectiveness of legal alternatives to avert the threat of nuclear war, we cited our own vigil at GTE, leafleting, letter-writing to GTE executives and to newspapers, shareholder activism, a legal protest in Washington, DC, that three of us had attended when Congress was voting on the MX, petitions submitted, candidates supported, articles, lobbying, art works, and books produced. We also cited our participation in the Nuclear Freeze movement and attendance at the United Nations first and second conferences on disarmament. On the effectiveness of prayer, we called Father Leo Barry to the stand and gave our personal testimonies as well.

After the prosecution and defense rested, Judge Tracy acquitted us of disorderly conduct and on trespass continued the case without a finding.

The next day, Dan Lawrence wrote his summary of the trial:

Dan Lawrence folds a prayerful banner.
photo by Tom Lewis

> It was utterly fantastic. I am still high a day later. To our surprise, Judge Tracy allowed us to use the necessity defense. He cut us off a lot at first, but as time wore on, he wore out and witnesses responded at greater length.
>
> The punch line of the whole thing for me is this: for three solid hours, everyone in the courtroom, which overflowed out into the hall, was showered with words on the hazards of nuclear war. It was unreal. I can't help but feel that Judge Tracy was perhaps caught off guard.
>
> Scott was terrific. You wouldn't believe it. He wasn't a rookie lawyer. He is a professional. He made the district attorney look like an apprentice. I tell you. God's presence was in that courtroom yesterday.
>
> My six co-defendants were beautiful. Sue was comfortable there right in her own town. And she was good and had a big impact. Michael was strong. He wasn't intimidated. War is bad, and Mike spoke it out in terms dear to parents. A sensitiveness came from him, a true concern for his children and the children of the world. He might have almost cried. He had to speak out. His insides were burning within. God, that man has strength.
>
> And Tom knew his assignment about nuclear firepower when Scott questioned him. He spoke so firmly. He deliberated, then spoke. No stuttering, no stammering. He spoke what he had to say, then stopped. Prophet of God. Man, no one trips up God. When that beautiful father of ours wants a message delivered, he/she can use raggedy muffins like Scott to turn the tables on black robes and stiff letters of court people or anyone else.
>
> Prophet of God Michael, Prophet Scott, Prophet Sue, Prophet Mary Laurel, Prophet Claire, Prophet Tom.
>
> Then the verdict without a sentence or fine. This is the first time this happened in the three years that we have been witnessing at GTE. Is it possible that we, to some degree, convinced the court that the danger of nuclear war is imminent? Did Judge Tracy feel we were right and so didn't sentence us?
>
> Yesterday, GTE was on trial for making missiles. They were being tried by Peace Witness at GTE. The trial didn't start out that way, but that is the way it ended up. Unreal. Unbelievable. But beautiful.

Interestingly, one of the tactics Claire and I often applied to promote nuclear disarmament is writing personal responses to those who had letters on the topic in the press. Back then, the newspapers printed the addresses of letter writers, making it easy to reach them.

After the *Worcester Telegram* published a pro-disarmament letter by a grandmother named Connie Riley, I wrote to her.

Dear Connie,

Peace! On behalf of the Peace Witness at GTE community here in Worcester, allow me to thank you for your wonderful letter to the *Telegram*. It was splendid, well-written, and to the point.

Our group has held a prayer vigil for peace outside GTE in Westborough for nearly three years every Friday from 3:30 p.m. to 5 p.m. (GTE does high technology work on the MX, Minuteman II, and Trident missile systems). We are busy writing letters, protesting, and urging legislators to vote for disarmament. My fiancée, Claire, and I spent the last year and a half in Washington, DC working for disarmament and, also, sheltering homeless men and women at two Catholic Worker houses of hospitality. Thirty-one people froze to death on the streets of Washington last winter, and the number three cause of Black infant mortality is rat bites. Black youth unemployment is forty percent, while sixty percent of adult Black males are either in jail or the military. The poverty is unbelievable and disgraceful as well, especially in light of military expenditures.

Since January of this year, there have been more people every day at the Pentagon calling for disarmament. Claire and I would go there to pray the Rosary and hold a sign: There is no way to peace, peace is the way, and another Pray for Disarmament. We feel it is very important to encourage as many people using as many non-violent methods as possible to act in their own ways against the arms race. We are uplifted by letters like yours. Please keep up your fine work for peace!

Shortly thereafter, Connie started attending the weekly GTE vigil. In unexpected ways, the community opposing the MX grew. The enthusiasm of newcomers buoyed the spirits of those who had protested at GTE since 1981.

Ellie Pepper, Sue Malone's best friend, also displayed enthusiasm. She came to many vigils and never failed to cheer us up with her smile. In 1997, her thirty-four-year-old son, Michael, took an ax and murdered Ellie and her husband John. *The Boston Globe* reported that Michael "had stopped taking anti-psychotic medications" and "Doctors who examined him said his mental illness affected his ability to tell right from wrong."

The double murder shocked everyone. It was a crushing blow to Ellie and John's three surviving children and to Sue. After Michael received a sentence of twenty-six years in a facility for the criminally insane, Sue became his only visitor. While many peace activists pay lip service to loving those who cause harm, Sue demonstrated that love regularly until her death in 2021. We knew Sue was special when she joined our protest at GTE, but her compassion for Michael Pepper proved she was more special than we ever imagined.

Hiroshima Day 1984

As weekly vigils continued, the Peace Witness at GTE planned an event for the Friday closest to the thirty-ninth anniversary of the US atomic bombings of Hiroshima and Nagasaki. We circulated a flyer beginning with the words on the memorial cenotaph inscription in Hiroshima for the A-bombs' victims: "Let all the souls here rest in peace, for we shall not repeat the evil." We called people to "Come with your banners and your peaceful spirits to the Friday Vigil at GTE on August 3, from 3:30 p.m. to 5 p.m."

Claire and I sent a letter to the director of the GTE plant:

> No one wants any more Hiroshimas, neither you—employees of GTE—nor us of the Peace Witness nor the people of the earth. But, as long as the danger of nuclear war exists and as long as corporations like GTE continue to engage in weapons design or production, we of the Peace Witness intend to continue our prayerful vigils for peace. We bring our prayers and symbols to GTE as an act of hope, not of despair. We invite all GTE employees to join us at any of these vigils—now, before a global Hiroshima happens—and we express once again our wish and desire to be in constant communication with you.

On the morning of August 3, Ernestine LeBeau, a fifty-one-year-old schoolteacher and single mother from Framingham; Dan Lawrence, Claire Schaeffer-Duffy (we combined our last names after our wedding), and I were arrested for kneeling in prayer a few feet into the GTE driveway. Our supporters held a banner across the street that read, No More Hiroshimas! Use your God-given talents for Peace!

We passed out the following leaflet:

> All told, more than 250,000 people were killed by the atomic bombs dropped at Hiroshima and Nagasaki on August 6 and 9, 1945. Most people know something of the suffering, but few know that many of the physicists and engineers who worked on the bomb's development argued against its use. In July of 1945, fifty-six members of the Manhattan Project wrote President Truman protesting on moral grounds dropping an atomic bomb on Japanese cities. They realized, at the eleventh hour, that the weapon they built to be used defensively against Hitler's army was going to be used without warning on Japan's civilians. The Manhattan Project workers argued,
>
>> If the United States were to be the first to release this new means of indiscriminate destruction upon mankind, she would precipitate the race for armaments and prejudice the possibility of reaching an international agreement on the future control of such weapons.
>
> Unfortunately, these nuclear scientists acted too late.
>
> This is why we are here today: to remind us all of the painful human toll that was paid for the work of scientists in 1945 and to appeal on our knees in prayer to you the new generation of nuclear technicians and engineers to say "NO!" now before it is too late. Remember, in 1945, we used every nuclear weapon we had. Today, that would be more than twenty-six thousand warheads, each with many times the explosive force of the Hiroshima bomb. This time will be the last time.

> For the love of God, for the love of life, we beg you, our sisters and brothers, to choose the path of resistance that so many of your colleagues have chosen. We've enclosed the testimony of one such man, Robert Aldridge, an aerospace engineer for nineteen years with Lockheed International.
>
> Monday and Thursday next week mark the thirty-ninth anniversaries of the bombings in Japan. Let us act now before that fate becomes the fate of the earth.

In a 1973 edition of the Catholic publication, *Pax Christi*, Aldridge's appeal "The Courage to Start," is a deeply moving and personal story of his conversion to the cause of nuclear disarmament. He tells how he was first challenged by his oldest daughter, Jane, who asked about protests at Dow Chemical over their production of napalm for use in Vietnam.

"I'm worried, Dad," Jane said to him, "Pretty soon the demonstrations will be against your work."

Ultimately, Aldridge not only left his work at the aerospace and weapons manufacturer Lockheed but also became a tireless opponent of nuclear weapons until his death in 2022.

Following Tom Lewis's advice that the anti-GTE campaign needed to gradually become more forceful, Ernie, Dan, Claire, and I opted to be tried by jury after our arrest for our 1984 presences at GTE, a choice that entailed greater preparation.

A judge might cut a *pro-se* defendant, one representing himself or herself, some slack during a two-hour-long bench trial but not during a likely much longer jury trial. Juries had to be protected by the trial judge from hearing inadmissible evidence. An error on our part could lead to a speedy conviction or a mistrial. We would also be tried in Worcester Superior Court, a more prestigious and intimidating venue. Although trial by jury is our Constitutional right, those who choose it and lose are likely to be jailed by busy judges who abhor frivolous cases.

All the factors raised the need to be well-prepared for that trial by a jury of six with one alternate. Misdemeanor charges do not qualify for a jury of twelve. I had to go back to the law library and read more decisions. We all had to recruit as many prestigious witnesses as we could. We had to find people considered authoritative if not expert in the area where we questioned them.

As in the case where we received no sentence, we planned a necessity defense based on the efficacy of prayer. To establish that element, we presented two Protestant ministers, Reverend Paul Ferrin, minister at United Church of Christ of Worcester and Reverend Stephen Harvester, pastor of the United Methodist churches of West Warren and West Brookfield. We also included the retired Roman Catholic Bishop of Worcester, Bernard Flanagan.

To establish that GTE's work on the MX posed an undeniable and imminent threat, we presented Katie Green, a GTE stockholder; Dr. Ted Conna, a psychiatrist treating adults and children who served as professor at University of Massachusetts Medical School in Worcester and co-director of Physicians for Social Responsibility; Dr. Tomas Winters, MD, assistant professor of occupational medicine at UMass Medical School; and our strongest witness, Dr. Paul F. Walker, a consultant in national security policy and Soviet-American relations, a military veteran, and one of America's most prominent experts on nuclear weapons.

To establish the failure of legal means to address the harm of the MX, we augmented our personal testimonies with a history of the disarmament campaign at GTE by Sue Malone.

We sent formal trial invitations to supporters and the press. Outside the courthouse, we passed out a four-page welcome filled with information about the MX and a bibliography of disarmament articles and books. We treated the trial not as a means to determine our guilt or innocence of petty crime but as a forum to evaluate and confront the threat of nuclear war.

A week after our arrest in August, the *Sunday Telegram* ran a profile of Sue Malone including a photo of her at a GTE vigil beside Ernie LeBeau holding a sign that read "ALL LIFE IS SACRED-WORK FOR PEACE." The article entitled "Would You Believe a Mother, a Nurse, a Church Organist?" had an italicized subtitle distinguishing Sue and Ernie from Tom, Dan, Claire, and me: "Not All Anti-Nukies Are Fanatic Crazies." Talk about a two-edged compliment!

Sue told the *Telegram*:

> Somebody, someplace, sometime has got to stand up and say, 'No, I won't do this anymore. I won't stand for this. As Ernie LeBeau said, "You can only talk about it for so long, and then people don't listen to you anymore. You have to take action because rhetoric is insufficient."

Dan Lawrence also got press. He told the Clinton, Massachusetts. *Daily Item*:

> "Love God and love your neighbor as yourself" are, for me, the two greatest principles to live by. They exclude murder. It's wrong. I feel called to promote life. Since I'm a human being, I am overcome a lot of the time, most of the time, by the seeming futility of my efforts. I continue because of interior fulfillment. To the extent that I am in union with the calling of my God, the results of my activities —whether great or nil—are unimportant.

Meanwhile, GTE was not standing idly by. On September 23, the Westborough facility ran a full-page ad in the *Boston Globe* under the heading, "C^3 Technology Isn't Standing Still. Why Should You?" Images of computer monitors next to a runner and bullseye irritated me as a long-distance runner. The ad ended with the following pledge to new employees, "We'll create the action. And then, let you run with it. As far as you want to go." Really? *No* limits on how far they wanted to go? In the context of GTE's exceptionally destructive contracts, giving engineers free reign seemed a chilling prospect.

The advertisement spelled out that GTE sought systems engineers in radio frequency communications, network design, space systems, data network design, knowledge-based systems, computer systems, software architectures, software development, and software systems. Could it be they had trouble holding onto their workers? Or, more concerning, were they expanding?

The trial for our Hiroshima Day demonstration began on November 7, 1984, with our introduction of a motion to employ a necessity defense. We supported the motion with a brief. Assistant District Attorney Harold Johnson moved that our testimony be restricted to the usual elements of trespass. Thankfully, Judge Thomas F. Fallon ruled against the prosecutor. Judge Fallon paraphrased Judge Paul Liacos, who sat on a 1983 trespassing case, *Commonwealth vs. Paul Hood* and who would serve as Massachusetts chief justice from 1989 to 1996. "If the defendant's right to have his day in court is to be guaranteed, he must be given the opportunity to establish even a tenuous defense."

A 1984 GTE ad seeks to attract systems engineers, network designers, computer programmers, and more.
clipping courtesy of Scott Schaeffer-Duffy

Then, both sides settled in to select a jury. After welcoming the members of the jury pool, Judge Fallon questioned each to determine if any needed to be excused for obvious conflicts of interest, biases, or other reasons. The defendants and prosecutor, armed with name, age, address, and occupation of each prospective juror, then asked additional questions. In some states, defendants and prosecutors submit such questions to the judge, who asks the queries he or she consider pertinent. In others, the prosecutor and defendants do so directly.

Both sides enjoy a fixed number of peremptory challenges, allowing them to exclude jurors without giving a reason. Once these challenges are exhausted, a juror can only be excused for cause by the judge, after revealing something serious enough to compromise them.

Years later, while on trial for a Martin Luther King, Jr. Day protest against the Trident Submarine in Groton, Connecticut, I asked a juror what she thought of protesters. When she replied, "I think they should be boiled in oil," I asked the judge to excuse her for cause.

But he asked the woman, "Do you think your opinion of protesters will hamper your ability to render a fair and impartial verdict in this case?"

When she replied, "No, your honor," and he said, "You may remain," I had no challenges left and was stuck with her as well as four other jurors who worked for General Dynamics on the Trident. To no one's surprise, *that* jury deliberated only *seven* minutes before finding me guilty.

Luckily, jury selection in Worcester did not turn out to be as contentious. The prosecution and defense easily agreed on a jury of three women and four men, with one later designated an alternate. An audience of fifty people filled the courtroom to see and hear the trial.

The district attorney's opening statement stressed that, by our own admission, we had violated the law and deserved to be convicted. He said, "The issue in this case is trespassing."

Ernie LeBeau opened for the defense by explaining necessity. She asked the jurors to find that "the circumstances justified our prayerful presence and that we are innocent of any wrongdoing."

The DA called Michael Augustine, superintendent of plant protection at GTE, and Thomas Higgins, a GTE security guard, to testify that we had entered GTE property without permission despite multiple, highly visible No Trespassing signs. When we refused to leave after being told to do so, Westborough Patrolman Joseph Crowe, who also testified, made two similar requests, warning that if we did not leave the property, we would be arrested.

Since we knelt down instead of leaving, we were arrested. To the DA, that evidence, which we did not contradict, provided straightforward support for convicting the four of us, and so, the prosecution rested.

We called Bishop Flanagan as our first witness. He described the United States Conference of Catholic Bishops' position that nuclear arms must be controlled. He then corroborated what he had said, "There are times and situations where civil disobedience is not only morally justified but may actually be a duty." He also stressed the unlimited power of prayer.

During cross examination, DA Johnson asked Bishop Flanagan, "Do you condone going onto someone else's property to make a statement?"

"It has to be left to the consciences of the people involved whether they are justified in breaking a lesser law, as it were, for a greater good," the bishop replied.

But then the prosecutor came up with an excellent question. "Do you believe that prayer off GTE's property would be as effective as prayer on the property?"

Taken aback, Flanagan hesitated before conceding, "Yes, it would. Prayer is effective wherever it is delivered."

Unfortunately for the DA, he went on to make a classic mistake when he asked our next witness, the Reverend Steve Harvester, the same question: "Do you believe that prayer off GTE's property would be as effective as prayer on the property?"

To everyone's surprise, Steve replied, "Absolutely not. In my pastoral experience, prayer is more efficacious in close proximity to the sick."

From the back of the courtroom, Bishop Flanagan said quite audibly, "I agree!"

The jury laughed, and Harold Johnson lost a well-earned point.

Then, the Reverend Paul Ferrin reinforced Steve's pastoral assessment of prayer.

Interestingly, before each of the defendants took the stand, I asked Dan if he had written out his testimony and he said, "No."

When I expressed surprise that he meant to speak without notes, he reminded me that in the Gospel according to Saint Mark, it says,

> When they take you and turn you over to the court, do not worry beforehand about what to say, but say whatever is given to you in that hour; for it is not you who speak, but it is the Holy Spirit who will speak through you.

And true enough, Dan's testimony, straight from his heart, delivered directly to the jury, proved very moving. So impressed was I at Dan's faith that I have never since read from a written text in court.

Paul Walker detailed for the jury the danger of GTE's work on the MX. He said, "the command, control, and communications, C^3, system of the MX missile was designed to fight a nuclear war before, during, and after a nuclear confrontation." Even if every human being had been incinerated, C^3 would keep firing nuclear weapons. He said the MX "increases the likelihood of nuclear war because it makes the nuclear trigger a hair trigger." Anticipating current fears about artificial intelligence, Paul went on to warn of the destabilizing impact of turning the launching of nuclear weapons over to computers.

Under cross examination Dr. Walker told the DA, "It is reasonable to believe that four people kneeling in prayer will affect defense policy." He punctuated his testimony with, "It is actions like theirs that have the MX missile in question now."

The testimony of Ted Conna, MD, mirrored comments he made to the *Catholic Free Press* before the trial began:

> It is the public's lack of awareness that is the greatest problem. I am testifying here today because it is the little I can do to help save the world. These people, the

defendants, are right, and I want to help raise people's consciousness so there can be a groundswell movement to get rid of nuclear weapons and survive.

With the first atomic bomb, we did not understand there would be radiation fallout, that the electro-magnetic pulse would disrupt all communication systems, that we would endanger the ozone layer—a mere three millimeters between ultra-violet rays that can destroy us. We didn't know about the nuclear winter that would be set off by the explosion of one percent of the fifteen thousand megatons of explosive power we have stockpiled in the United States and Russia. There would be so much junk in the atmosphere that no sunlight would be able to reach us.

He explained that such information increased depression and hopelessness, especially among children.

Clark Cardona, one of four students from Ernie LeBeau's class who attended the trial, confirmed Dr. Conna's point when he told the *Free Press*, "Nuclear weapons scare me. This issue pertains to us. It is an imminent social issue which, whether you agree or disagree, has to be brought up and discussed on all sides."

A second student, Thomas Roskey, told the *Free Press*, "What Mrs. LeBeau did makes me step back and take a look. I usually think 'they're nothing but peace protesters—lock them up.' This time, it is our English teacher, whom I always thought was pretty straight."

With tears welling up in her eyes, Ernie testified that, on the morning of August 3, as she knelt in the GTE driveway, she held an enlarged photo given to her by a survivor of the atomic bombing in Hiroshima. Her voice cracked as she described the picture of "an incinerated child."

She told the jury, "I was frightened for my own children, my flesh-and-blood children. I have two, and I was frightened for every child that I ever taught."

She went on to say that she grew up wondering about why more Germans did not resist the Holocaust and feared that companies like GTE were preparing "a much bigger and much ghastlier holocaust."

"This was a very difficult thing for me to do," she testified under cross examination. But I had to go where this genocide is being prepared. This, to me is legal, as God is my judge."

Claire Schaeffer-Duffy also spoke with clarity. "Our defense is one of necessity that holds, after finding legal means insufficient to abate the immense harm imposed by the work going on at GTE on first-strike weapons and other nuclear technology, that we had a reasonable belief that in appealing to the intellect, compassion, and souls of the GTE workers we could attempt a conversion of outlook."

As in our previous trial, we all introduced numerous ineffective previous actions we had taken to abate the harm of nuclear war. We each made it clear that civil disobedience was a last resort. After that, the defense rested.

Judge Tracy instructed the jury that they could consider what he called the "choice of evils" defense, but only if the jury believed we had conclusively proven its required elements.

"You have heard each of us speak from our intellects, from our hearts, and from our spirits," I told the jury in closing. "We would ask you to find us innocent of criminal charges on this day."

"This is not a philosophical question, not a religious question, not a question of nuclear war," DA Johnson said. "The defendants have made a very eloquent case, but that's not the issue. I suggest that no one in their right mind wants to see nuclear war, but that's not the issue in this case."

With dramatic effect, he described us. "Well intentioned? No question. Moral? Perhaps. Religious? Apparently." Then, after a pause for effect, "But guilty."

In a precedent-shattering trial, GTE protesters lose a battle, but perhaps win a war

Defendants (left to right) Ernestine LeBeau, Dan Lawrence, Scott Schaeffer-Duffy and Claire Schaeffer-Duffy argued that the threat of nuclear destruction justified their illegal presence on the grounds of GTE Corp. in Westboro on August 3.

PHOTO/PATRICK O'CONNOR

photo by Patrick O'Connor • November 10, 1984 in *Worcester Magazine*

Arguing the single matter at issue was whether or not we were guilty of trespassing, the prosecutor went on to point out that GTE only manufactures components of the MX missile. "On a table at GTE, does that component present an imminent threat to anyone? The imminent threat the defendants are talking about has nothing to do with GTE in Westborough. These people have interfered with the use of a citizen's property. If you begin to abandon people's property rights, where does it end?"

After deliberating for three hours and to our disappointment, the jury returned guilty verdicts for all four of us. DA Johnson recommended six months' probation, but we told Judge Tracy that we could not in good conscience promise to obey the law "as long as preparation for nuclear war goes on." The judge set us free for the weekend and scheduled sentencing for the following Tuesday. As Claire left the courtroom, she told *Worcester Magazine*, "Someday soon, the verdict is going to be not guilty."

On Tuesday, the judge sentenced Dan and me to 15 days in jail. He initially sentenced Claire and Ernie to $77.50 each in fines and court costs, but when they both said that paying any money would be an admission of guilt, he gave them 15 days in jail as well.

Interestingly, during the men's confinement in Worcester County Jail and the women's in Massachusetts Correctional Institution, MCI, Framingham, the *Catholic Free Press* published the following letter:

> I've been a subscriber to the *CFP* for about ten months. I've never written a letter to the editor, but Dan Lawrence's November 1 letter (from jail), "the menace to society," just screams out for rebuttal.
>
> As the product of eighteen years of Catholic education, I was taught that the ends never justify the means.
>
> Dan's actions are possibly understandable. He probably missed saluting the flag, Vietnam, and the anti-Communist speeches I listened to in my Catholic school. I think Dan is getting off lightly with just an arrest from GTE and the submarine base in Groton, Connecticut. If Dan is not happy with the USA, its laws, and his seven-thousand-dollar-a-year wage, his options are open.
>
> What bothers me much more is the attitude and direction of your newspaper. The published word has a very strong influence on the average reader.
>
> Your newspaper encourages dissent, civil disobedience, and disregard for the law. I believe you must admit that if you are honest with yourself.
>
> Cancel my subscription.
>
> Roger Tremblay

While some people supported our civil disobedience for disarmament, many, especially cold-warrior Catholics, did not.

Because our sentence was so short, Dan and I were never classified to go to minimum security. Six hours after our release from jail, Dan told the *Worcester Telegram*, "The worst thing for me was the denial of freedom and the constant noise."

I can vouch for Dan's comment. One morning in the cell we shared, I woke up to find Dan writing with intensity. When I asked him what he was doing, he said, "I'm writing a letter to the sheriff."

"What about?" I asked.

He handed me the letter written after an inmate escaped and dogs were posted outside the maximum-security area as deterrent to others. It read:

> Dear Sheriff Deignan,
>
> For the last two nights, there have been dogs running loose outside the lower left tier of maximum security. The dogs are making a terrible racket. There's enough noise in here as it is. Get rid of the fucking dogs.
>
> Peace and Love, Dan Lawrence

Taken aback, I said, "Dan, don't send this letter."

"Why not?" he asked.

"You can't swear in a letter to the sheriff," I explained.

"Why not?" Dan replied, "Everyone around here, guards included, use swears in every sentence. I think that's the way they communicate in here."

So, Dan sent the letter and consequently spent the last two days of his sentence in the hole, solitary confinement in a windowless punishment cell. Ironically, I think Dan, the former Trappist monk, preferred it to maximum security.

In a December 2 *Worcester Telegram* article on Ernie's jail experience, she said, "I thought it would be something of a monastic period, a time for deep thought. Instead, I never had a second to myself. The emotional drain was enormous."

The article described the jail routine:

> Part of her days in the module, a barracks-style room that houses short-term prisoners, were spent cleaning toilets and scrubbing floors. She also devoted hours to talking with other inmates, including Mrs. Schaeffer-Duffy. Ernie and Claire often gathered quietly in a corner at the far end of the module, where they set up folding chairs and prayed together. Sleeping was difficult because the lights were kept on twenty-four hours a day.
>
> "It's clean, and the guards are kind. I think everyone working in the prison tries to do the best they can," Ernie offered before saying, "I thought I was ready, but I don't think anyone is ready for prison."
>
> The hardest part of her prison stay, she said, was seeing what she called the inequalities of the judicial system. She blamed those inequalities for the high percentage of undereducated and uneducated minorities she said were in the jail. Many of the women, she said, were there because they could not pay a fifty-dollar fine.
>
> Mrs. LeBeau credits her teenage daughter for providing needed support and insight during her prison stay. "All along, she said to me, 'You've got to follow your conscience.'"

Ernie spent her first day home reflecting on her prison stay.

"And I really thanked God for the experience. I spent the rest of the afternoon quietly looking out the unbarred windows."

Mrs. LeBeau said she was afraid her arrest might complicate her teaching position at Marian High School, a co-ed Catholic school where she had taught English for four years.

But she discussed her plans to protest with the school's principal, a nun, before her arrest. She also discussed the possibility that she might be imprisoned for up to thirty days if found guilty of trespassing.

Mrs. LeBeau recalled the principal's reaction.

She said, "They would never do that to you. They would never put you in jail for praying for peace."

Mrs. LeBeau readily admits that she could have avoided her prison term and the disruption it caused in her life by paying a $77.50 fine.

"It was a matter of conscience. I felt paying the fine was tantamount to saying "Yes, this was wrong. It was not wrong," said Mrs. LeBeau.

In a letter written from the county jail to the *Worcester Telegram & Gazette* published on December 17, I said:

A prison official, who remembered Tom Lewis and my previous stay here for a similar protest at GTE, told me, "Why, we're going to have to build a civil disobedience wing soon. We'll call it the Thoreau Wing."

Dan, Ernie, Claire, and I are heartened and indeed filled with hope by the growing numbers who care enough about the future to risk their freedom in the present.

The jail sentence we serve now is not an end to our efforts for a conversion of GTE and places like it to peaceful work. This prison retreat is another seed of a future harvest of peace and justice.

A Parental Appeal and More

Three months earlier, on September 17, 1984, I sent the following letter to Worcester Catholic Bishop Timothy Harrington, who had been appointed by Pope John Paul II after Bishop Flanagan retired in 1983:

Dear Bishop Harrington,

Peace! I am a member of the spiritually based group, Peace Witness at GTE, concerned that a spirit of nonviolence can be engendered in all aspects of life. We are greatly encouraged by the statement of Cardinal Joseph Bernadin, Archbishop of Cincinnati, saying that the issues of the arms race, abortion, and capital punishment should not be separated but seen in the light of a "seamless garment" respect for life.

In this context, I was pleased to see your statement in the September 14, 1984 *Catholic Free Press*. I believe you did well to list the various concerns, but I was distressed to see that the *Free Press* and the *Worcester Telegram* emphasize only abortion. In the present political context, this amounts to an endorsement of Ronald Reagan and a tearing of the Seamless Garment. The *Free Press* devoted only fifteen words to your comments on nuclear weapons and did not even mention capital punishment, while the *Telegram* gave all the other issues only one sentence buried deep in the article.

I was happy to see that the United States Conference of Catholic Bishops' pamphlet, "Political Responsibility: Choices for the 1980s," was well balanced but sad to see only Cardinal Bernadin articulating carefully the absolute inseparability of the various life issues. I urge you to make a more public correction of the stress of both articles and to preserve your prophetic role as non-partisan teacher.

We are praying for you and your efforts on behalf of the sanctity of life.

On September 24, Bishop Harrington replied, "I assure you of my commitment to the broad range of life issues which face us today. Your commitment to life challenges me. I thank you. With blessings and best wishes."

Two days prior to the bishop's letter, the Peace Witness at GTE, sent a letter to the twenty GTE workers for whom we had addresses and GTE executives but hoped our letter would be passed around the plant.

While the weekly vigil could communicate a few words on a sign or banner, letters and leaflets afforded us the opportunity to say more. We opened with a quote from the prophet Jeremiah, 31:15, "In Ramah is heard the sound of moaning, of bitter weeping! Rachel mourns for her children. She refuses to be consoled because her children are no more." The text is read at Mass every December 28. In the opening paragraph of our letter, we explained why:

> December 28 marks the Feast of the Holy Innocents. This day signifies an observance of the time when King Herod slaughtered all male Jewish children under the age of two in Bethlehem. Rumors of the Messiah's birth threatened the secular king. To assuage his fear, he killed the innocent.

We went on to make a personal appeal as parents ourselves, knowing that many GTE workers also had children or planned to do so:

> For those who are parents or expectant parents, this day is a time to reflect upon the vulnerability of children in the nuclear age. Every day, five to ten new nuclear weapons are added to the already existing arsenal of between forty thousand and fifty thousand warheads. A child born today has five chances in a thousand to reach adulthood, according to *Year One*, November 1984.
>
> The children know they look to a fragile future. American Psychiatric Association sponsored surveys of children's attitudes on nuclear war that document their fear. One study of over a thousand sample students, conducted by Harvard psychiatrists Dr. William Beardslee and Dr. John Mack between 1978 and 1980, "suggest that children are deeply disturbed about the threat of nuclear war."
>
> Most of the children questioned knew of the nuclear bomb before they were twelve. A more recent study of students, ages eleven to nineteen, reveals that children's

expression of fear and helplessness and anger toward the adult generation have increased over the last four years. If the missiles are launched, we will not be able to protect the young from the blasts or radiation, and, even now, we cannot shelter their minds from the despair that follows a child's awareness of nuclear death.

Unlike Rachel of ancient days, the modern Rachel and her husband must shield their children from a Herod of their own making. As adults, we have planted seeds that have yielded a harvest of MIRVs, MARVs, ICBMs, SLCMs, and C^3. Children will not survive in this garden. For every 1.3 million dollars spent on the military, thirty children die for lack of food or inexpensive vaccines. The US Command Control Communications system provides no guidance for a child; its sole purpose is to guide a warhead to a place where other children might dwell.

The children look to us, who give them life, to reassure them. The studies cited above say, "It is therapeutic for children to perceive their parents are actively working to prevent nuclear war."

We offer some specific suggestions on how you can carry on this work and inspire hope amongst children.

We suggested three books, including Dr. Seuss's *The Butter Battle Book*. We suggested they read it to children and then ask them how they would resolve the conflict the book presents. We also recommended they leave GTE and join our weekly peace vigil.

The letter was signed by:
    Scott and Claire Schaeffer-Duffy for an unborn child due in June
    Matthew Shorten and Rose Carrier for Karina Carrier Shorten
    Cherie Grant for Lori, Donald, and Eric Grant
    Maureen Halden for Matthew Halden
    Sam Shoaff and Mary Donnelly for Andrea and Katherine Donnelly
    John and Mary True for an unborn child due in May
    Frank Kartheiser for Kendra and Alexandra

While Bishop Flanagan was a progressive intellectual, Harrington was a blue-collar cleric devoted to the poor. I first met him in 1977 on the loading dock at the Catholic Charities warehouse on Sycamore Street in Worcester. At the time, he was Worcester's auxiliary bishop, an office that didn't stop him from stripping down to a white T-shirt and helping unload heavy bundles of clothing from a delivery truck. Although Harrington was not a leader on nuclear disarmament, he did not stand in the way of diocesan offices that continued to pursue peace and justice.

On January 11, 1985, the *Evening Gazette*, reported, "GTE Diversifies Its Contracts." Clare Deveney, manager of GTE public affairs, announced that the strategic systems division in Westborough had won contracts to work on the Minuteman nuclear missile and the US Ballistic Missile Defense program as well as the MX. She said, "We would be hopeful that Congress would release additional funding for the MX program. We expect those votes to be quite close."

She also said that third quarter profits for GTE were $3.6 million, eight percent higher than the year before.

Two days after publication of the report, the *Evening Gazette* ran a letter from Dan Lawrence entitled, "MX Funds Should Go to the Poor."

Six days after Dan's letter appeared, *The Voice* ran an editorial by the editor, Mary Donovan, defending the use of the necessity defense by Peace Witness at GTE. She quoted Thomas Jefferson who, when asked, "Is it ever right to break the law?" replied:

> A strict observance of the written laws is doubtless one of the high duties of a good citizen, but it is not the highest. The laws of necessity, of self-preservation, of saving our country when in danger are of higher obligation. To lose our country by a scrupulous adherence to written law, would be to lose the law itself, with life, liberty, property, and all those who are enjoying them with us; thus, absurdly sacrificing the end to the means.

Ms. Donovan also quoted Thoreau regarding his refusal to pay federal taxes in opposition to the US invasion of Mexico, a war he believed was imperialistic and promoted the expansion of slavery: "Must the citizen ever for a moment or in the least degree resign his conscience to the legislator? Why has every man a conscience, then? I think that we should be men first and subject afterward."

Undoubtedly, our campaign to disarm GTE, even though it had thus far been unsuccessful, continued to stir minds and hearts. Indeed, a letter I wrote to David Lange, prime minister of New Zealand, praising his decision to prohibit nuclear-armed ships from entering their ports, was answered promptly with a personal reply: "Thank you for your letter. It is heartening to have your support for the New Zealand Government's anti-nuclear policies."

Forty-Day Preparation for More Civil Disobedience

In the words of Monty Python, we thought, "Now, for something completely different."

We had prayed in the GTE driveway twice, poured blood once, and used the necessity defense twice. For Good Friday 1985, we decided to ramp up our outreach and attempt a different Catholic approach to GTE workers.

The outreach began in late January when we wrote to the pastors of numerous parishes in the Diocese of Worcester asking them to publish in their bulletins an invitation to join the weekly prayer vigil at GTE "as a Lenten offering for 1985." After detailing the harm of nuclear weapons, our letter said, "Surely prayerful action must be our response to the military machine. If the Christians remain silent, then who can be expected to speak for peace in these times?" We attached a sample bulletin announcement with directions to the vigil and an offer for rides.

To our delight, Father George Rueger, pastor of Worcester's Saint Peter's Church, ran an "Invitation to Vigil for Peace" in the bulletin on February 17, February 24, and

March 3. Father Jim Mongelluzzo, pastor and rector of Saint Paul's Cathedral, went even farther. He not only advertised the GTE vigil throughout Lent but also added on March 2, 1985:

> Peacemaking is not an optional commitment. It is a requirement of our faith. We are called to be peacemakers, not by some movement of the moment but by Our Lord Jesus. The content of our peacemaking is set not by some political agenda or ideological program but by the teaching of His Church.

On the Third Sunday of Lent, March 9, 1985, Father Mongelluzzo followed the Peace Witness at GTE invitation with selections from the American Catholic bishops' pastoral letter, "The Challenge of Peace, God's Promise and Our Response." He said the bishops

> fear that our world and nations are headed in the wrong direction. Nuclear weaponry has drastically changed the nature of warfare, and the arms race poses a threat which is without precedent to human life and human civilization.

Claire and I sent a letter on March 28, to GTE executives and workers notifying them of our upcoming action:

> On Good Friday/Passover, several members of the Peace Witness will once again come prayerfully onto the property at GTE in Westborough. The end of the Lenten season and Passover coincide this year on Friday, April 5.
>
> On the day Jesus died, and the Israelites were freed from slavery, we will come to GTE. We do this because, while forty-two thousand children starve to death each day, in the same twenty-four-hour period, the US spends more than nine hundred million dollars on the military! In the face of crying human need, our nation allocates ever more of its material and human resources to build nuclear weapons. And the Command Control and Communications, C^3, system, to which GTE contributes, will not only guide these weapons to their millions of human targets but will continue to do so, even after every American is already dead.
>
> We see C^3 as a sin for which we share the awful responsibility. By our taxes, commerce with nuclear weapons manufacturers, our violence within and without, and our failure to resist this evil, we have acquiesced to the mass murder of our sisters and brothers. In light of our complicity, we want you, the workers at GTE, to know that we will celebrate the Sacrament of Penance. During that Rite of Reconciliation, we will ask God's forgiveness for our violence and nuclear sin. On Good Friday/Passover, we will come to GTE to confess our guilt and to beseech God for the grace to turn from all violence to love. As always, you will be most welcome to join our prayer.

As you might imagine, stints in jail can disrupt family life and jobs. Tom Lewis went to great lengths to secure employment that respected his sojourns behind bars, but even sympathetic employers might not be able to carry on without hiring a replacement. Possibly losing one's job added an element to consider when deciding whether or not to risk arrest.

I held a part-time job at a group home for mentally challenged adults. In solidarity with the poor, I insisted on being paid the minimum wage, an arrangement that allowed the state Department of Mental Health to hire another part-time staff member. Perhaps, due to that arrangement and to my good work record, I did not feel that civil disobedience imperiled my job.

I couldn't be so sure about a part-time position I held at the Rainbow Child Development Center. The nursery school, located inside one of Worcester's public housing clusters, needed every worker every day. Most of the adorable children came from single-parent households. Working at Rainbow gave me a deep awareness of the importance of regular commitment to those children.

On Wednesday of Holy Week, two days before Good Friday, I wrote a letter to my boss at Rainbow, telling her about the GTE prayer/protest. In that letter, I said,

> I firmly believe that those who care enough to work with small children would naturally oppose the nuclear arms race. My wife, Claire, and I are expecting our first child in June, and we want that child to grow and live in a world safe from the horror of a six-minute nuclear war.

Would it be enough? I'd have to wait and see. While it might sound easy to proclaim as Martin Luther did, "Here I stand. I cannot be otherwise," losing a beloved job or, worse yet, letting needy children down is painful.

When added to our fear of nuclear war, day-to-day concerns at work and home compelled us to devote ourselves to preparing protests that warranted the risks we took. Those who think repeat offenders, as I had become, found civil disobedience easy mistook dedication for ease.

And so, each participant in the Good Friday witness at GTE took great pains to write a leaflet that actually said something to the workers rather than just some self-serving blah blah blah. Our earnest desire to do what was right, bumped up a bit by God's grace, enabled us to write more carefully. The 1985 Good Friday leaflet offered:

> On this night many centuries ago, Israelites offered the blood of a spotless lamb so God might be moved to pass over and free them from slavery and death. In a similar way on this day, Jesus offered his own flesh and blood for the forgiveness of sin.
>
> Today, all humankind is weighed down by a sin so ghastly we can scarcely comprehend it—the willingness to incinerate all life on the planet. But we will not despair. The death and resurrection of Jesus, like the Passover and Exodus, show us that violence will not have the final word. Neither Pontius Pilate nor Pharaoh could squelch a faith that is willing to suffer and to take on guilt rather than lay the blame. The seemingly eternal cycle of recriminations, anger, hatred, and war is broken only by the willingness to say, "I am responsible. I am sorry. And I will try, with God's grace, to love more fully." For many followers of Jesus, this mystery of Divine Healing is made visible in the Sacrament of Reconciliation.

Our candid admission of guilt and celebration of God's forgiveness is a beginning. From such a starting point, we hope to move toward a relationship with our enemies based not on threats and self-righteousness but on humility and love."

Early in the morning on April 5, 1985, eight of us got dropped off just outside the GTE main lobby where we displayed a banner reading, "Lamb of God, you take away the sins of the world, grant us peace."

Wearing a purple stole, Father Bob Branconnier, a sixty-year-old associate pastor at Saint Matthew's Church in Dorchester, a neighborhood of Boston, opened the Rite for Reconciliation of Several Penitents with Individual Confession and Absolution.

Tom Lewis, Dan Lawrence, Claire, and I were joined by Mark McCarthy, a twenty-five-year-old carpenter and student at Worcester State College; Daniel Sicken, a forty-three-year-old appliance repairman from Brattleboro, Vermont, who had been arrested six times before for anti-nuclear civil disobedience elsewhere; and Dan Ethier, a twenty-six-year-old graduate of the University of Minnesota, who had recently left a job as a software engineer at Data General Corporation to work in a shelter for homeless families and was a graduate student in religious studies at Assumption College.

We opened our prayer singing, "Ubi caritas et amor, ubi caritas, Deus ibi est," translated from the Latin as "Where there is charity and love, there is God also." We performed an audible examination of conscience to determine our sins followed by a litany led by Dan Sicken, prayer by Dan Lawrence, and intercessions by Claire. Then,

Eight witness at GTE on Good Friday, 1985, in a Sacrament of Reconciliation.
Their banner reads "Lamb of God, You take away the sin of the world. Grant us peace."
ink on paper by Tom Lewis • April 12, 1985 in *Catholic Free Press*

each of us privately confessed to Father Branconnier, who followed by making his own confession to us all.

It felt oddly liberating for me on my knees at GTE to offer the same Act of Contrition I memorized for my first confession at Saint Theresa's Church in Blackstone, Massachusetts. Words in prayer books seem livelier in the open air. Although I didn't feel even slightly more attracted to knocking on strangers' doors to talk to them about religion, referring out loud to a God "good and deserving of all of my love" while surrounded by armed police officers in the shadow of a sleek weapons plant seemed profound. Interestingly, perhaps because some of the police were Catholic, none of them made a move to arrest us until our prayers were completed.

Eventually, the usual routine commenced. Plant security and local police asked us to leave. When we did not, they arrested us and took us to be charged, fingerprinted, and photographed. At the police station, Claire told a reporter for the *Catholic Free Press*, "We were able to confess our guilt and complicity in the arms race and be forgiven before we were arrested."

Then, we were taken to Westborough District Court to appear before Judge Brewin, who said, "You are obliged to comply with the civil law which gives you the right to exist. With your actions, you are not being good Catholics."

Nonetheless, he offered to release us until our trial six days later on April 11 for a hundred dollars cash bail or a thousand dollars surety.

Dan Sicken, Father Bob Branconnier, and Claire Schaeffer-Duffy listen during arraignment for their Good Friday action at GTE.
April 11, 1985 photo • *The Voice*

"Judge Brewin, would it help you to know that we do not intend to make bail?" Father Branconnier asked.

In consequence, the judge offered to release us on personal recognizance, but only if we would promise to obey the law, something he already knew we would not do.

Then I said, "We all wish to enter guilty pleas."

Instead, as a matter of judicial prudence, Judge Brewin entered not guilty pleas on our behalf, advised us of our right to an attorney, and sent the six other men and me to Worcester County Jail, and Claire to MCI Framingham to await trial.

That afternoon, the *Catholic Free Press* featured the reactions of Worcester's current and retired bishops. The Most Reverend Timothy Harrington said:

> If Jesus was anything, He was a man of peace. The protesters at GTE are convinced Christians who are willing to put themselves on the line, risking jail and ridicule, for what they and many others believe in.
>
> People say that nuclear war is impossible, yet we stockpile weapons in our country as we neglect women, children, the handicapped, and the aged among us who need help. One does not buy an umbrella unless one is expecting it to rain at some time.
>
> We forget that the people who make munitions in this country, like the people on welfare, are on the public dole. Not all of us are able to participate in acts of civil disobedience, but we all are able to pray and to let our consciences be pricked by actions such as the Good Friday GTE protest.

Bishop Flanagan offered:

> In view of the recent actions of Congress approving twenty-one new MX missiles, it would seem demonstrations such as the one at GTE are of even greater importance in raising our consciousness to the perils we face in the continuation of nuclear arms escalation. For a growing number of people, peaceful nonviolent demonstrations have become an accepted way to give witness to their opposition to the arms race and their deep concern for the awesome danger it implies to the world. I can only hope their willingness to stand up for their convictions will help others to realize the perils involved in our present course of action and add to the ranks of those willing to fight for peace through disarmament.

Interviewed before his arrest, Dan Ethier said, while working across the street at Data General, "I would see the people vigiling at GTE each week, and I wondered who they were and what they were doing."

Well, after our Good Friday action, Dan had first-hand experience of who and why.

Over Easter weekend and the following week, the three Dans, Tom, Father Bob, Mark, and I enjoyed six hours a day together outside our cells. Father Bob celebrated the Eucharist each night after dinner, Tom sketched, and I commented—in jocular reference to our jail time pending trial—that I'd been to many other priests who gave easier penance after confession.

Claire, approaching the eighth month of her pregnancy in a time when smoking was still allowed in jail, had it much harder than we did.

Upon his release, Mark told the *Middlesex News*,

> I didn't know how to present myself in jail, whether to be tough or not. The first night, I went directly to sleep because I was afraid, but after that, I wasn't afraid of anyone. The worst that happened was that someone made it clear he didn't want to talk to me. I felt good about (the jail time) all the way through. It strengthened my convictions.

On April 11, we were brought back to court, where we discovered that Judge George Sullivan would hear our cases. Because we did not contest the charges, he quickly found us guilty.

Without the censure we experienced in front of Judge Brewin, Judge Sullivan sentenced us to time served. Shortly thereafter, we gathered with friends and supporters in the lobby to offer a prayer of thanksgiving, and Judge Sullivan surprised us all by coming out in his robes and standing just outside the prayer circle with his head bowed.

Father Bob Branconnier celebrates Mass in a Worcester County Jail cell.

ink on paper by Tom Lewis • May 6, 1985 in *The Voice*

The following day, a letter entitled "Peace" appeared in the *Catholic Free Press*, which said it had been sent from Worcester County Jail by Scott Schaeffer-Duffy, Claire Schaeffer-Duffy, Robert Branconnier, Daniel Ethier, Jane Lewis, and Dan Lawrence. I marveled at how Mark had disappeared from the line of signatures, that Claire had somehow made it into the men's jail, that Father Bob's name was reimagined, and that Tom Lewis became female. Interestingly, there were no typos in the text about the Easter triumph of life over death.

Father Bob had a letter to the editor in the following week's *Free Press* saying, "Thanks for the dedication and competence you bring to your work as editor of what is one of the best diocesan papers I have seen." A week after that, the *Evening Gazette* ran a letter I sent from jail. As in previous instances, the press gave our actions considerable attention.

The media didn't win everyone over to our point of view. We received an anonymous letter that concluded:

> In World War II, good Americans took up arms to kill a marauding beast, not to maim or mutilate. Then we had distance between us and the threat. Now we don't. We have only seconds. Because a police officer is armed does that make the officer a killer, mutilator, etc. because the firearm has that destructive potential? Our nuclear defense potential is similar, except the six bullets are more like 60 million. If we disarm the officer, will criminals stop using force to rape, rob, maim, or murder?

The writer's references to C^3 led me to suspect he or she worked at GTE. In handwriting below the typed text, the author wrote, "Sincere thanks for the opportunity for each of us to understand." I wish they had provided us the opportunity to reply.

Claire and I were surprised when Bishop Harrington sent us a letter on June 20, 1980, three weeks after the birth of our first child, Justin. He wrote,

> Congratulations on the birth of your baby Justin. Continue to shower him with love. His coming into your lives is contrasted dramatically with the birth of children on the streets into homes of violence. When you pray daily with and for Justin, remember the children of the world. Best wishes and God's blessing.

In her reply, Claire thanked the bishop and invited him to join us on August 9 at GTE to mark the fortieth anniversary of the atomic bombing of Nagasaki.

Bishop Harrington answered on July 2:

> I am not prepared to be with you on August 9. I, however, shall be addressing a pastoral letter to the people of our diocese, noting the fortieth anniversary of the bombing of Hiroshima and Nagasaki. The remembrance of that holocaust is our challenge for peace. Your journey in peacemaking is your witness. God be with you. Your peacemaking has become front page news in praise, not in conflict. That is beautiful. Be assured of my prayers for you and your extended family of peacemakers.

Unexpected Consequences

Sometimes, civil disobedience wasn't our idea. There were, and still are, many local, national, and international organizations working for nuclear disarmament. When one of them asked us to collaborate, we did our best to do so. On July 12, 1985, the New York-based Mobilization for Survival made an appeal for simultaneous demonstrations at nuclear weapons installations throughout the United States between August 6 and 9 to mark the fortieth anniversary of the atomic bombings in Japan. We took up the challenge and began planning another civil disobedience at GTE. Given the short notice, we didn't have time for months of brainstorming, so we settled on something simple. A group of us would get dropped off again at the main entrance and kneel holding signs commemorating the atomic bombings and calling for nuclear disarmament. Encouraged by the relatively short jail sentence we received on Good Friday, I thought I could manage the time away from Claire and our newborn son, Justin.

As our evangelical neighbor, Reverend Doug Dyer, used to tell me, "You know how you make God laugh? You tell him your plans."

We chose to demonstrate on August 9, the anniversary of the atomic bombing of Nagasaki, because that fell on our regular vigil day. Nine people agreed to risk arrest: Dan Ethier, Dan Sicken, and I, joined by Connie Riley, a mother of eight and grandmother of five from Gardner; Ann Sorensen, 53, the outreach director at Mount Hermon School, from Northfield; Deirdre Doran, 28, from Jamaica Plain; Mary Jane Rosati, 35, from Boston; Paul Giaimo, 23, a recent graduate of Holy Cross College, from Worcester; and Mark Johnson, 33, of Spencer. It was a nice mix of women and men, young and older, newcomers and veterans.

On August 8, *The Worcester Telegram* ran an article entitled, "Protest to Mark Anniversary of 'Forgotten Bomb' at GTE" in which I said that nine of us would enter GTE property early on the next morning and about fifty would vigil that afternoon. I explained that the Nagasaki bomb was more reprehensible to me than the Hiroshima bomb because it was unnecessary. When President Truman learned that the Japanese might surrender before the second A-bombing scheduled for August 11, he moved it up to the ninth. He told the *New York Times* that we had many atomic bombs and would keep dropping them on city after city until the Japanese surrendered unconditionally. Actually, we only had two bombs but looking ahead to the cold war with the Soviet Union, we wanted to scare them and any other potential adversaries. The people in Nagasaki were killed for geopolitics.

Unlike previous protests, we gave the media advance notice of our plans, not because we considered press vital to the effectiveness of our protest, but because the Mobilization for Survival urged organizers to do so. When asked by the press if we wanted to be arrested, I said, "Not one of us has any great desire to be arrested. My wife, Claire, and I have a newborn son to think about."

Also on August 8, Paul Giaimo told *The Catholic Free Press:*

> It is not often recognized that the protest of nuclear arms has been ongoing since their development forty years ago and it will be ongoing until they are no longer a reality. With our presence, we are hoping to make the workers inside the plant aware of their role in GTE's growing part in the continuation of the nuclear tragedy. Our action is done at the risk of imprisonment and out of love as we humbly confess our own weakness and invite GTE workers to join with us in the hard work of bringing about the disarmament of weapons and hearts.

Paul Giamo, left, kneels during August 9, 1985 protest at GTE while Michael Augustine, GTE security officer, observes and Connie Riley stands in resistance.
photo by Donna Hartman

That afternoon, *The Fitchburg-Leominster Sentinel and Enterprise* (one of many local newspapers that no longer exists), ran an article entitled, "Gardner mother and peace activist to join in protest at Westboro plant." Connie Riley, the co-chairperson of the Peace and Justice Committee of the Montachusett People's Action Committee, told them, "We risk going to jail not only to protest forty years of the nuclear arms race, but also to celebrate forty years of nonviolent action for disarmament."

Connie had come a long way from just writing letters to the editor.

In our Nagasaki Day leaflet, we opened with Bishop Harrington's assessment of our civil disobedience: "The miracle of life demands your witness for peace." We went on to describe protests against nuclear weapons, going back to 1948, culminating in 1982 when 750,000 people marched for nuclear disarmament and 1,800 committed civil disobedience in New York City. We concluded the leaflet with:

> Our persistent efforts at GTE celebrate and continue the rich history of disarmament work. Our action today is one of more than forty acts of civil disobedience around the country to mark these forty years. We invite your participation in this story. It will take the hands, hearts, and minds of many to create a world where a Nagasaki or a Hiroshima will never happen again.

A GTE security officer arrests Scott Schaeffer-Duffy on August 9, 1985.
photo by Donna Hartman

Holding signs, with photos of atomic bombing victims, that read, NO MORE NAGASAKIS, NO MORE VICTIMS, and THE MX CAN DO THIS, we were told by GTE security officer Michael Augustine, "I am asking each of you to leave on your own accord. You are trespassing." Since none of us left the property, we were arrested by Westborough police.

As spokeswoman for the Peace Witness at GTE, Claire, holding our infant son Justin, told T*he Middlesex News*, "We want to help the workers at GTE realize the fruits of their work. They tend to separate their work on the MX and a whole city being obliterated."

When we appeared that afternoon in Westborough District Court, Judge Brewin arraigned us and then offered to try us immediately. Since defendants who were dissatisfied with the result in Westborough had the right to appeal in Worcester, we agreed.

The trial began on a good note. In his testimony for the prosecution, officer John Perkins said, "The early morning protest was very peaceful."

Later, when I testified that Nagasaki's Catholic Cathedral was Ground Zero for the atomic bombing, Judge Brewin interrupted, "Thank God. I wouldn't be sitting here today if Harry S. Truman, a great man of courage and vision, didn't save millions by dropping those two bombs."

Later, as I described how Paul Giaimo and I had been praying the rosary prior to our arrest, Judge Brewin jumped in again with, "That's an admirable deed. I pray for peace every Sunday. We all want peace, but there is a place to state your cause. It is at Congressman Joseph Early's office or at the White House or at Senator Edward Kennedy's office. It is not your right to make a speech in this courtroom."

After Connie Riley explained that she joined the protest because hungry and homeless American children need the money spent on the military, Judge Brewin retorted, "Children are dying of starvation because the defense budget is too large. But you have the right to free petition without trespassing. Get a permit. Have a rally."

I later learned that two of Judge Brewin's siblings fought in World War II. One may even have died in the war. Perhaps that background influenced his impatience and disagreement with us.

After the very short trial, Judge Brewin found all of us guilty and sentenced Dan Sicken and me to the maximum, thirty days in jail plus $140 in fines and fees. Others were given suspended jail sentences and fines and fees between $65 and $140. When seven of us said we could not in conscience pay any money, though, for personal reasons Mark Johnson agreed to pay the fine. Judge Brewin told us that if we did not pay the fines, we would work them off at $3-a-day in jail, a formula that has long since been discarded.

"You hold the key to your own incarceration in your own hands," he added. While it's gross hyperbole, it wouldn't have shocked me a bit if, like Pontius Pilate, he had asked for a bowl of water and washed his hands of us.

Counting the time for refusing to pay fines, the sentences were: seventy-seven days in jail for Dan Sicken and me, fifty-seven days in jail for Deirdre Doran, forty-seven days in jail for Dan Ethier and Ann Sorenson, who said she would appeal, while Mary Jane Rosati, Paul Giaimo, and Connie Riley received twenty-two days in jail.

After I called the unexpectedly long sentences "terribly unjust," the nine of us joined hands and began to pray.

Judge Brewin banged his gavel and shouted, "Order in the court! You'll do that downstairs (in the holding cells) if you want to. This is not a church!" Despite his opinion, most of the courtrooms I've been in, including Judge Brewin's, look remarkably like modern churches without stained glass windows. I think both institutions do their best to focus attention on a robed individual elevated above the audience.

When I calculated my jail time, I thought, "Yikes! This is more than double any previous sentence."

Claire kept the focus on GTE. She told *The Gardner News*, "GTE is the largest nuclear weapons contractor in central Massachusetts. They are developing the guidance system for the MX and other first-strike weapons systems and have recently obtained a contract for the Star Wars program."

In a jail interview with *The Catholic Free Press*, which ran on August 16, Connie Riley also kept her composure saying, "I used my body to block the entrance to GTE. If enough of us protest, we can stop the arms race. We must not remain silent."

That same edition of the *Free Press* ran a letter from the two Dans, Paul, and me from Worcester County Jail. We encouraged readers to write to the women imprisoned in Framingham and to continue to attend Friday vigils at GTE. We added, "While we have no desire to be in jail and appreciate the feelings of those who are upset by the jail terms, we want it clearly understood that we are not angry or upset. As the letter of Saint James tells us,

> Consider it pure joy, my sisters and brothers, whenever you face trials of many kinds, because you know that the testing of your faith develops perseverance.

The next day, *The Worcester Telegram* published another letter I sent entitled, "Truman Had Alternatives to the A-Bombing of Japan." Secretary of War Henry Stimson's appeal for President Truman to hold off A-bombing Japan until the expected declaration of war by the Soviet Union on August 15th, something Stimson believed would lead the Japanese to surrender immediately. I also quoted Pacific Fleet Commander Admiral William Leahy, who told Truman, "The Japanese are already defeated and ready to surrender because of the effective sea blockade." I finally noted that the Japanese emperor had already offered to surrender if he were allowed to retain his office (something the United States ultimately agreed to), and that Supreme Allied Military Commander, General Dwight Eisenhower said, "Japan was, at the very moment (of the atomic bombings), seeking some way to surrender with a minimum loss of face. It wasn't necessary to hit them with that awful thing."

The deluge of letters to Worcester area publications about nuclear weapons didn't stop there. Theresa Fichtel had a pro-atomic bombing letter, entitled "Do Japanese Mourn Pearl Harbor Dead?" On the same page of the *Telegram,* Mike True, Mary Healey, and Michael Hachey had different letters condemning nuclear weapons and supporting those of us in jail.

How did Connie, the newcomer to civil disobedience, fare? On her release from MCI Framingham, in an interview with the *Sentinel-Enterprise,* Connie said being handcuffed was "scary" and jail was "the most frustrating place you can imagine," but the sentence was "in a way, symbolic because this country is held hostage by the bomb and we, in turn, are being held hostage by the government." Regarding overcrowded and noisy conditions in Framingham, she joked, "I think I finally found a way to save money on my vacation." She concluded on a more serious note with "The people in Germany during World War II had crematoriums in their backyards and there was a stink, but they went about their jobs as usual. I think people will begin to realize that we have a stink in our backyard, and we can't ignore it."

We enjoyed absurdly numerous opportunities to further promote nuclear disarmament. Those of us in Worcester County Jail had no inkling how quickly our situation would deteriorate.

That deterioration began within minutes of our shuffling off the transport vehicle in the jail's sally port. On the ride over, after Paul expressed some trepidation, I advised him, as Tom had me, to lay low and ease into the jail experience. Unfortunately, Paul was an expansive, very friendly person.

"Can you buy me a pack of cigarettes?" another inmate asked him.

Paul replied in a very audible voice, "No problemo. I have lots of money on my books."

All too quickly, other inmates started asking Paul for more items until one very burly guy said, "Aren't you the dude who owes me two cartons of cigarettes?" Things escalated until, during the three hours we had each day out of our maximum-security cells, I saw a shirtless and muscle-bound guy named Julio poking Paul in the chest with his index finger while saying, "I can put this finger right through your body. Wanna see me do it?"

Seeing my terrified co-defendant, I interrupted, "Hey, Julio. Are they going to open the gym today?"

Forgetting Paul, he turned to me and answered, "I don't know, man."

Luckily, the next morning, the two Dans, Paul, and I were transferred to minimum security on the third floor or a former nurse's dormitory. The light blue walls, normal windows, polished wooden floors, and relaxed guard who sat at a teacher's desk gave Paul the impression we had gone to heaven. He didn't even mind the fact that nine bunk beds were squeezed into the space.

The bathroom was bright and clean, and we enjoyed a couple of hours of outside rec time in an unfenced area with a basketball court and a baseball field surrounded by trees. Paul went from a man laden with anxiety to an inmate who could, as the saying goes, do his jail bid standing on his head.

On our second day in the outside yard as I ran the perimeter, inmate after inmate told me in a low voice, "Rosario's split." Not exactly sure who Rosario was or where he went, I said nothing.

When we got back to the third floor, everyone expected the guard to raise Hell when he did his count and realized that Rosario had escaped, but the corrections officer, CO, merely jotted down the results in the daybook, picked up the wall phone, and called them in.

"He's pretty cool about things," I marveled.

But three hours later, when the CO did the last count before lights out, he shouted, "Where's Rosario?" Apparently, he hadn't noticed his absence earlier.

Suddenly aware that the guard would be in trouble for effectively giving Rosario an enormous head-start in his flight to freedom, guys flipped over pillows, looked under beds, and checked in the toilets while they said sarcastically, "He's not in here. He's not in here."

As bullshit as the CO appeared about the teasing, he looked more concerned when he called downstairs to the deputy. I wondered if the guard would be reprimanded or even fired.

In no time, two other guards came into the dorm, emptied Rosario's locker, and looked through his mail. It didn't take long for them to discover letters from a girlfriend in Worcester's Great Brook Valley apartment complex.

Evidently, most escapees make a beeline to their lovers. As they expected, the police discovered Rosario in his girlfriend's arms before the clock struck midnight. By that time, he could have been hundreds of miles away, but instead Rosario received extra jail time that he'd finish entirely in maximum security.

The very next day, Friday, August 17, the first-shift CO proved to be young and good-humored. Completely at ease with all the men, many whom he knew by name, the guard leaned back in his chair and joked like we all were his best buddies.

At three o'clock, after the congenial guard left, the CO, still-in-the-doghouse for screwing up the previous day's count, came in and shouted, "Where's the guard book?"

It took only a minute for an inmate to find it sitting in less than an inch of water in a toilet. Evidently, one of the men, caught up in the previous CO's bonhomie, had tossed it there. The vinyl-covered book suffered no damage, but the new CO did not care. He made a call downstairs and then grimly announced, "There'll be no visits, outside rec, phone calls, television, or commissary until someone comes forward to admit doing this." When no one confessed, he then told us to get together and find out who did it,

His words struck home. Almost immediately, several men pointed a finger at a timid nineteen-year-old who spent most of the time hiding under the covers in his top bunk. While I assumed the prank had been pulled off by an immature inmate, I had no doubt that that guy couldn't be the one. Effectively, the men offered up the person least able to defend himself.

I grabbed my copy of the sixteen-page rights and rules book, given to every inmate on arrival, and waved it aloft saying, "Wait a minute. The rule book says the COs are required to conduct an investigation and then hold a disciplinary hearing for anyone accused of breaking a rule. We shouldn't turn anyone over."

I figured the tension could be dialed down if we could talk to a deputy instead of the guard who was probably still pissed at us for razzing him the day before, so I walked up to the desk and said, "Excuse me, officer. We would like to see a deputy about this situation."

With his arms folded across his chest, the CO said, "You're not talking to nobody." It took all my self-restraint not to correct his use of a double negative.

One of the inmates complained, "They treat us like dogs."

In another attempt to calm things down, I opened the rule book to page two and read, "You have the right to expect that, as a human being, you will be treated respectfully and impartially by all personnel."

I went on to read:

> Disciplinary action shall be taken only at such times and in such measures and degrees as is necessary to regulate inmate behavior within acceptable limits. So as not to compound the inmate's problem by referring it to the Disciplinary Board for formal action, line staff are encouraged to counsel with the individual regarding his problems in an effort to avoid the necessity of formal action.

When the guard continued to ignore us, I said to the men, "Let's start a hunger strike until we can see a deputy to resolve this fairly."

An appalled inmate asked, "You mean not eating?"

Changing course, I suggested, "Well, if not that, we can refuse to work."

That resonated. We each had minuscule daily chores like emptying the trash or sweeping the floor. Refusing to do them wouldn't exactly throw the jail into chaos, but it might get a deputy to sit down and talk with us.

I quickly wrote a short proposal, which everyone signed. Then, Scott Palmeri, doing six months for breaking and entering, and I were elected spokespeople. I gave the petition to the guard, who sent it downstairs.

Ten minutes later, a CO poked his head through the door and yelled, "Palmeri! Schaeffer-Duffy! The deputy wants you downstairs now!"

Since such a meeting required proper dress, I grabbed my blue denim button shirt to put on over my white t-shirt, but the guard stopped me with, "No. Come as you are."

He then turned to the others and asked, "Anyone else want to go downstairs?"

Dan Ethier stepped forward.

When Dan Sicken started to do the same, a suddenly shocked Paul grabbed his arm and pleaded, "Don't leave me here alone!" so Dan stepped back.

The guard took the three of us down and sat us on a bench outside the deputy's office. After a couple of minutes, the CO waved me inside, where I discovered a room in pitch darkness. I was ushered into a wooden chair, and a bright light came on from a goose-neck lamp pointed right into my face. It felt like being interrogated in an old B movie. I could see only the edge of the deputy's desk and the shoes and lower legs of the guard behind me. It did not bode well.

Things looked up when the deputy spoke and I realized it was Larry Meershman, someone I'd gotten to know and like in my previous time at the jail. When I had told him that my Uncle Walter's funeral was scheduled for 11 a.m. on the day of my release, he made sure I got out at 7 a.m. sharp. Surely, he would see that the CO upstairs had made a mountain out of a molehill.

Before I could say a word, though, Larry asked, "Do you take responsibility for the work stoppage upstairs?"

I replied, "I think this situation is easily resolved. I can explain."

He merely repeated, "Do you take responsibility for the work stoppage?"

"We all agreed together," I said.

"But do *you* take responsibility?" he persisted.

A nanosecond-second after I answered, "Yes," the guard behind me stood me up, removed the chair, put me in handcuffs and leg irons, and shuffled me away in front of wide-eyed Scott and Dan to a waiting van. Shortly thereafter, similarly chained, they joined me.

On the short ride to maximum security, Dan and I agreed to fast until our rights were restored. Scott just thought we had no choice but to take whatever punishment awaited.

Once we reached the main building, guards escorted Dan and Scott to cells in upper right maximum security. Me, however, they took to a side hallway with six cells known as county lockup. Those windowless cells each had a toilet and steel bunk with no mattress, pillow, or bedding, like The Crowbar Hilton. Unlike police station cells in Westborough, though, the temperature in county lockup could not have been higher than fifty degrees.

I bitterly regretted not wearing my long-sleeve shirt.

The guards told me we would appear on Monday before the disciplinary board to face charges for

> Inciting a riot, encouraging others to refuse to work, conduct which disrupts or interferes with the security or orderly running of the institution, participating in an unauthorized meeting or gathering, and attempting to commit any of the above offenses or aiding another person to commit any of the above offenses or planning to commit any of the above offenses.

The disciplinary overkill reminded me of *Alice in Wonderland*, where the Queen of Hearts says the same thing to every prisoner: "Take him away! Off with his head!"

The next forty hours made it clear to me why Allied prisoners in the sixties television show *Hogan's Heroes* called punishment barracks "the cooler." Try sleeping on cold steel. I took small comfort from Saint Matthew's Gospel that says, "The Son of Man has nowhere to lay his head."

Before I could devolve into rampant self-pity, though, the inmate in the cell opposite mine shook me up. He laughed off every privation and boasted of how he had polished the aluminum band along the edge of the bars of his cell so he could watch TV reflected from the guard station down the hall. He also demonstrated how he could coil toilet paper loosely and set it on fire on the toilet seat to warm his cell. I forget what creative means he used to start the fire.

His jovial attitude demonstrated how ingenious and indomitable human beings could be. He reminded me of Gene Wilder in *Stir Crazy* who tells the warden, when he comes to get him out of solitary confinement, "So soon? I was just starting to get in touch with myself."

Whenever I complained, my cell-block neighbor said, "This ain't so bad," or "It could be worse."

Perhaps his optimism gave us good karma, because on Sunday morning a guard asked us if anybody wanted to go to Mass. Along with Mr. Cheerful and me, an inmate who did merit a mattress and bedding was on suicide watch. Another inmate sat on a chair outside his cell to make sure the other guy didn't kill himself. Typically, prisoners awaiting a D-Board did not get to go to the chapel, but the particular guard took whoever wanted to go. Meanwhile, Dan, locked up in maxi lower left, was denied his right to attend Mass.

Enroute walking to the chapel with a slow-moving line of other inmates, I spotted a priest I already knew and asked him if I could make a phone call.

"Sure," he answered and gestured to his small office a few feet to my left.

I took the opportunity to call Claire and briefly describe our circumstances. When I told her to call the bishop and the press, the priest overheard me and said, "That's enough phone time."

I don't think jail chaplains get a lot of slack from the head honchos.

Outside of that prayerful hiatus, Dan and I stewed in county lockup until Monday morning, August 19, when we were taken individually to another windowless room and sat down before a beefy captain who read the charges.

When finished, he asked, "Do you have anything to say?"

He then, repeatedly interrupted my five-minute testimony with "Is this germane?" "Are you finished yet?" and "Can we get this over with?"

It was pretty clear that the pro forma hearing left no doubt of the outcome. I had no counsel present, could not call witnesses, and saw that the proceedings were not being recorded.

When I asked about the right to receive visitors, the captain said, "That's where you're wrong. You're a ward of the state; a prisoner. You have no rights." (Alongside a letter I wrote describing the hearing, *The Catholic Free Press* quoted Deputy J. Paul Deignan who said our request to see a deputy about the book-in-the-toilet prank was "potentially dangerous. If the situation had not been controlled, it would have spread like fire throughout the rest of the building." He also said he was present for the hearing, an outright lie. And it was not true that I had been told I have no rights).

After I offered to show the captain the pages in the Handbook for Inmates delineating our rights, he asked, "What do you do for a living anyway? Are you a lawyer?" He then told me that rights were conditional on obedience to jail rules.

I said, "I can understand where privileges like contact visits and work release are conditional, but aren't rights by definition unalienable?"

He said rights were "forfeited when rules were broken."

Amazed at his stubbornness, I replied, "Then, my co-defendant Dan Ethier and I have no choice but to fast and pray to promote human rights in this jail."

"Fine," he jeered, "you can do that for thirty days in lockup."

Since the guards didn't want us instigating any more protests, they put Dan, Scott, and me in different tiers of maxi. We could talk to other inmates through the bars of our cells but could not leave them for any purpose. We were locked in twenty-four hours a day,

Although the *Handbook for Inmates* assured, "You have right to freedom of religious affiliation and voluntary religious worship," we were not taken to Mass. A guard agreed we had the right to send mail, but, by breaking jail rules, we had forfeited the privilege to buy pen, paper, and stamped envelopes from the commissary. Luckily, my neighbor, a guy called Deebo, passed me materials to write to Claire.
When I finished the letter, I handed it back to him, and he put itmin between two of his own outgoing letters.

As helpful as Deebo had been, I came to hate the fact that, late at night when the entire tier was locked in, men from all over the place shouted every few minutes, "Hey, Deebo!"

His standard reply, "Yo, wuss up?" didn't lead to fruitful conversation, just more cries of "Hey, Deebo!" But at least I had bedding and wasn't freezing.

I was hungry, though. A guard came by my cell three times a day with a meal, but I only accepted the orange juice and cartons of milk. Routinely, the CO would tell me, "Why don't you eat? Your buddy in lower right is eating."

Thankfully, while the jail didn't seem to care about human rights, it did worry we might starve ourselves to death, so they started sending Dan and me to the infirmary every other day for a check-up. As luck would have it, we went at the same time, affording us the chance to confer. I learned that Dan had, in fact, not broken the fast. He also told me that a man named Bob in the cell next to him on lower left had attempted suicide by slitting his arm, something he later told Dan he had done to get medical attention for nerve damage in his hand. Both of us, though, felt pretty good and were prepared to go without solid food for the entire thirty days locked up.

After Father Tom Flemming was denied the right to visit Dan and me on August 20 and complained to the chancery, word began to circulate on the tier that Bishop Harrington would be allowed to visit the next day. The novelty of anyone coming to see us in our cells prompted an inmate, two cells to the right of mine, to start boasting how he'd embarrass the bishop with a blizzard of sexual comments.

On the day Harrington came, he entered the tier and noticed the boastful guy locked in while other cells, save mine, were open, prompting the bishop to approach and inquire, "I see you're locked up. Is there anything I can do for you?"

His solicitousness so disarmed the tough inmate that he replied in a low voice, "Not really. Thank you for asking."

Harrington, a blue-collar guy who grew up in Worcester, never forgot his roots. In fact, after giving me Communion through the bars and learning that Dan and I were well, he said, "I'm glad to hear it, but hope you can appreciate that I can't ask for either of you to get special treatment, like an early release. If I did that for you, I'd have to do it for everyone."

Long before Black Lives Matter, Bishop Harrington refused to kowtow to white privilege. Although I would have been pleased to get out of lockup, I appreciated his integrity.

After visiting Dan and me, Bishop Harrington sent a letter of "personal concern" to Claire and Justin, our two-month-old son. He wrote,

> I realize that you are sustained and strengthened by your common bond and your pursuit of peace for the world. Your marginal resources must be overextended. I am enclosing a personal gift to support you. Be assured of my prayers for you.

Below this typed letter, he added a hand-written account of his visit to the jail:

> Today, I saw Scott. He looked well and in good spirits. I met with him and Dan Ethier. From Scott's description of how he landed in lock-up, it was a situation which got out of hand. Scott saw to it that a weakling in the group, who was being made a scapegoat, did not get assaulted by the others. He and another prisoner were elected spokesmen and as such were judged as the cause of what might have turned into a riot. The latter is the judgment of the corrections officers and administration. In prison, it is a different world. The last thing those in charge want is letting the prisoners get the upper hand. Dan Ethier just got caught up in the flow of things. I'll go again to see the non-GTE fellow (Scott Palmeri).
>
> I also visited Dan Sicken and Paul Giaimo. They were glad to get news of Scott and Dan.
>
> I hope things are well with you. I know "a new baby" means work and work, especially when you are tired. If the burden gets heavy, let me know, please.

Despite the bishop not seeking special treatment for Dan and me, the sheriff must have been moved by the episcopal visit because, on August 22, Dan and I were escorted to the office of Deputy Andrew Looney (his real name, no kidding) to learn that we were released from lockup. Dan would be moved to my tier. They told us we'd be transferred to minimum security as soon as possible. We agreed to end our fast and hoped to rejoin Dan Sicken and Paul.

On August 23, Father Rueger from Saint Peter's was allowed to bring all four of us Communion. I don't know if he got into MCI Framingham where the women were imprisoned.

Two days later, the *Middlesex News* ran an article entitled, "To Westboro N-Arms Protesters, Jail Is Freedom." Indeed, Deirdre Doran told the paper:

CIVIL DISOBEDIENCE — Deirdre Doran, left, and Mary Jane Rosati are serving sentences at MCI-Framingham for trespass-

August 25, 1985 in *Middlesex News*

This is great freedom for me. I accept the jail experience. We have exhausted all our legal means of preventing nuclear war. Civil disobedience frees others. I consider peace work and resistance my occupation. I am attempting to live below the taxable limit. I like to joke about living on the lunatic fringe.

Since the article had to be written earlier, it said Dan Ethier and I were "confined at the jail for disciplinary reasons and could not have visitors. Deputy Sheriff Looney would not elaborate on the weekend incident that led to their confinement."

In the same article, Mary Jane Rosati said,

It's hard for my family, because they feel if you go to jail you are a criminal. It's still really an experiment for me. But if jail is the price you have to pay, then I will pay it.

She told the reporter that she expected to be arrested again on September 14 protesting the Trident submarine in Groton, Connecticut.

Paul Giaimo spoke in the *Middlesex News* of the liberating effects of civil disobedience achieved by Jesus, Martin Luther King Jr., Mahatma Gandhi, and Henry David Thoreau. He said. "As a Christian, I believe there are forces more powerful than nuclear arms and destruction. I am acting on my faith and out of my conscience."

Dan Sicken told the press that he would probably lose his job at an appliance repair company but could still do repairs on his own. He said,

I don't feel hopeless or helpless about nuclear war. With our witness, we testify to the imminence of nuclear war and the importance of people engaging themselves in direct action. I am one day going to be held accountable by God for my actions or inactions in these dangerous tines when conscience doesn't seem to be emphasized enough.

Three days later, after vomiting twice and feeling flu symptoms, Paul asked to see a nurse. When he was told he'd have to wait twenty-four hours, friends paid his fine and took Paul to Saint Vincent's Hospital. He ended up bed-ridden for two days.

On August 17, Dan Ethier had a letter printed in the *Worcester Telegram* in which he said:

ACTING ON CONSCIENCE — Daniel Sicken, left, and Paul Giaimo are serving time at Worcester County Jail in West Boylston for their part Aug. 9 in an anti-nuclear arms protest at the GTE Strategic Systems Inc. plant in Westboro.
(News Photo by Donna Hartman)

August 25, 1985 in *Middlesex News*

> During testimony (at our trial), Judge Brewin interrupted to tell us that if Truman had not used the atomic bombs, he might not be here today. He believes those bombs saved his life. I believe Judge Brewin is a victim, with many World War II veterans, of the lie that claims the atom bomb was the only way to force Japan to surrender. The evidence tells a different story. Japan offered to surrender as early as April 1945 if we would allow them to keep the emperor.... The incinerated victims of Hiroshima and Nagasaki and the Americans killed in combat during May, June, and July were the first pawns of the cold war.
>
> I bear no grudge against Judge Brewin for sending me to jail. He is a victim of this lie. I am keeping him in my prayers, just as he promised in court to pray for us. I hope he will also join me in praying for an end to the arms race.

Dan's letter ran alongside one from R. Jay Allain from Northampton who called the A-bombings an "unspeakable atrocity."

Gary McCaslin and Bernard Kaplan from Worcester also wrote letters. Gary argued, "The challenge of 1985 is to register the danger of the vast nuclear arsenal, change our way of thinking, and dedicate ourselves to building a world where life on earth can continue."

Bernard commended May Healey, Michael True, and me for our letters and said, "One ought to be able to recognize evil wherever it occurs and not participate in the delusion that the United States and its leaders are alone guiltless in the world."

Also on August 30, Connie Riley had a letter in the *Boston Globe* identifying herself as "a sixty-three-year-old grandmother" urging everyone to "fight proliferation of weapons of death" by writing to President Reagan and Congress.

Later that day, Deirdre Doran had a letter in the *Evening Gazette* in which she concluded:

> We act in hope that others will take responsibility in disarming the weapons of omnicide. We are encouraged by the success of non-violent direct action throughout history, which has freed people and enhanced the quality of life.

The avalanche of letters continued in the next edition of the *Evening Gazette* where Mary Jane Rosati said:

In my work as a registered nurse, I foster health care and life-sustaining activities. One only has to read Carl Sagan's work on nuclear winter to realize how anti-life this weaponry is. My three beautiful young nephews deserve to grow up and prosper in a nuclear-free environment, freed from wondering where the bomb may actually be used. I ask all of you who love this planet to please write your congressperson or the president and to join a group working for peace in your area.

On September 8, as we still waited to go to minimum security, a man came onto our tier for disciplinary lockup. He hopped on one foot while demanding to see a doctor. He explained to Dan Ethier that he injured his foot while in the Deignan Building and believed it was broken.

He said he was taken to lockup for refusing to stand for the count, something he could not do with his injury. A nurse told him there was nothing wrong, but he continued to ask to see a doctor, which he did on September 9. The doctor sent him for X-rays which confirmed that his foot was broken in three places. Nonetheless, the disciplinary charges were not dropped, and he was returned to lockup.

The next day, Dan Ethier and I were moved but not reunited with Dan Sicken. Instead, guards escorted us to a medium security wing. Maxi consisted of a two-story block with back-to-back cells facing a corridor and barred windows. Unless you were on lockup, each cell housed two men, one on a steel bunk and the other on a mattress on the floor, a kind of tight squeeze. Other prisoners told me that each cell used to have two bunks welded into the wall, but after a court agreed with an inmate lawsuit that challenged the two-bunk per cell arrangement, the jail took out the second bunk and continued the practice in a way not covered by the lawsuit.

You can't make this stuff up.

Medium security amounted to a building that also had two floors with cells facing each other across a corridor that ran down the middle. What made it medium instead of maximum is that each cell had only one inmate. While in many ways that was better, I would soon learn how it could be very much worse.

On the day they moved us, I carried my mail, toothbrush, soap, and notebooks. Typically, when a prisoner was moved, the guards shouted their name and yelled, "Bag and baggage!" That meant taking everything—clothes, towels, and linen. If you got moved without those items, the bureaucracy would take forever replacing them.

Dan's guard, unlike mine, had him bring everything, which Dan arranged in his cell at the far end of the tier. I stood at the opposite end with my hand on the bars as I called down to the corrections officer at the first-floor guard station, "CO, I need bedding!" So focused was I on not returning to fruitless attempts to sleep while frozen that I didn't notice another inmate come up to my left side. I just continued trying to get the guards' attention.

The guy next to me, though, looked at my left hand and asked, "What kind of ring is that?"

Without turning his way, I said, "It's an Irish wedding ring."

He replied, "Do you want to sell it?"

Preoccupied by my need for linen and tired of unending jail drama, I glanced his way and said, "Take a fucking wild guess," and continued yelling, "CO!"

A couple of hours later, after getting clean sheets and a blanket (the squeaky wheel sometimes does get the grease), I noticed that the guy whom I swore at locked in his cell across from my own.

I walked up to the bars and apologized. "I'm sorry I swore at you earlier. I'm pretty exhausted."

He immediately reached out, grabbed my head, and began smashing it into the bars while screaming, "You swore at me!"

Only then did I realize that this guy was six or seven levels beyond tightly wound.

After I broke free, he learned from another inmate that I was a pacifist. The information inspired him to ask me in scenario after scenario if I'd kill him or someone else.

"What if an asshole threatened to stab you? You'd kill him then, right?"

"No," I said *ad nauseum*.

But nothing satisfied him. He kept ratcheting up the hypothetical situations. "What if a Nazi was about to kill a dozen babies and you had a gun?" "What if someone was about to push a button to destroy a city?" "What if I tried to kill another guy on the block?" "What if I tried to kill you?" And finally, "What if I was going to rape and then kill your wife?"

Talk about crossing the line.

Barely containing my anger, I said, "My wife is a devout Christian. She wouldn't want me to risk separating myself from her for all eternity by committing the mortal sin of killing you."

When he still went on, I said, "Look, I'm a pacifist. I won't kill you but, with all the racket you are making, I can't promise one of the other guys in here won't kill you."

Up until meeting that psychopath, I had prided myself on saying that I never met a prisoner in jail whom I would not take home with me, but that jerk spoiled the boast.

To Dan's and my dismay, the bad news kept mounting. After someone on our tier punched Rosario of the short-term escape fame, administrative lockup became the order for the entire floor. Since it happened on the weekend, officials did not assign a deputy to begin the investigation. The administration denied the innocent along with the guilty their right to religious worship, visits, recreation, and phone use.

Around 5 p.m. on Sunday, I told the officer in charge, "These guys are all pretty mad about being locked up so long when all but one of them is innocent of wrongdoing. If you keep everyone locked up, I'm afraid they'll do stupid things."

The CO replied, "And they'll get more lockup time for that, too."

I retorted, "True, but only because they were provoked by an unfair lockup. This policy is inciting a riot."

The guard said with sympathy, "I know, but I don't make the rules. When I get oak leaf clusters and captain's bars, I'll make waves and not until."

My concern proved correct. Not long after my conversation with the guard, men began shouting and lighting small fires in the corridor. Mr. Crazy, across from me, assembled a particularly large bonfire, and when he put two aerosol cans on top of the pyre, both my neighbors warned me to put my mattress against the bars and hide behind it or risk getting hit by shrapnel.

Great. Things just got better and better.

After flames and smoke built and two surprisingly loud explosions burst out of the fire, guards sprayed a hose down the length of the corridor, thus putting an inch of water in every cell. Undeterred, the inmate from Hell plugged his toilet with a towel and began flushing it over and over until water began rising everywhere. With maniacal laughter, he screamed, "You want water! I'll give you water!"

Instead of returning to remove the culprit, the guards chose to innovate. Apparently, the water in our floor was leaking down onto the tier below, ruining the photos men had attached to their cell walls with toothpaste. The guard chose the biggest and angriest inmate down there, brought him up to our tier, and set him loose. This guy looked for the wettest cells, which turned out to be Dan's and mine, due to unevenness in the floor. He pointed his finger at each of us in turn and announced, "Your number is punched."

After he departed, the odious inmate across from me laughed his head off.

My neighbors warned that we might get "bundled."

Not sure I wanted to know, I asked, "What's that?"

"When you are walking to chow or the gym, someone will throw a blanket over your head and men will stab you over and over until the blanket is completely soaked with blood."

Not much sleep that night, I assure you.

While nothing happened the next day, everyone told us to keep on guard. Then, miraculously, Bishop Harrington heard of our plight somehow and paid the balance of Dan's and my fine, getting us released on our thirty-ninth of seventy-seven days.

Dan Sicken finished the jail time on his own and generously never blamed Dan Ethier and me for getting out early.

But we could not forget those inmates still suffering in that too often lawless jail, so Dan and I sat down and looked through our journals and recorded all the abuses we witnessed. We then arranged a meeting with Deputy Sheriff Deignan to cite abuses and ask for reform.

He listened to us quietly and then asked, "How do you know that these things are still going on in the jail?"

"We just got out a couple of days ago," I reasoned.

"They may all have changed by now," he said without mirth.

When I asked if he would allow us or an independent group of legal observers into the jail to verify respect for inmate's rights, he refused.

In other words, if inmates gather to object, it's an illegal meeting. If former inmates complain, they no longer have standing. If observers seek access, it will be denied. Effectively, the jail was a closed world free without consequence to treat people as its staff and administration liked.

While nuclear disarmament remained our primary goal, we could not let that nonsense go on unchecked, so Dan and I wrote a report on conditions entitled "Thirty-Nine Days at the Worcester County Jail and House of Corrections," which prompted *Worcester Magazine* to run a cover story on the jail's injustices. Following that coverage, the magazine published a letter from me saying:

> One of the most difficult aspects of being in jail is the sense that what you are experiencing is something completely secret. Hopefully, public awareness will help prevent further abuses. Dan Ethier's and my seventeen-page report not only details forty-one specific abuses but also makes eighteen concrete suggestions for improvement. As our introduction clearly states:
>
> > The following pages are not offered to scapegoat anyone who works at the jail, but to afford the entire staff concrete suggestions on how they might better implement the rights and policies described in the *Handbook for Inmates*.

As Christians, though, Dan and I felt compelled to go beyond mere suggestions for jail reform. Our conclusion recalls the early Church's refusal to support courts or prisons and questions the morality of punishment as a means of achieving reform. We believe Jesus came to proclaim freedom to captives and a message of reconciliation, forgiveness and love so deep that it extends to the most heinous enemies. We tried to remind our non-Christian siblings on the jail staff of the jail's own code, but we call the Christians to take the counsel of the early Church:

> The Christian must bind no one, nor imprison any. It seems clear to us that in a nuclear society where the death penalty, nuclear and conventional arms, abortion, and life-threatening poverty are completely legal, the people of conscience, especially the Christians, should be nonviolently breaking these laws rather than enforcing them.
>
> Anyone who would like a copy of our report, please send $1.00 for printing and mailing costs.

Meanwhile, the weekly peace vigil at GTE continued unabated in increasingly cold weather.

Valentine's Day Reimagined

On the snowy morning of February 14, 1986, Carol Bellin, a thirty-two-year-old media technician from Somerville who joined an eight-thousand-mile peace walk in the US, Western Europe, and the Soviet Union, and I got dropped off near the eight-foot high, silver and blue, triangular GTE sign on which Carol splashed our own blood before we unfurled a red banner with a white lace heart encircling the words "Love Disarms."

A GTE security agent stands by as Carol Bellin, left, and Scott Schaeffer-Duffy assert that love disarms during a February 14, 1986 demonstration at GTE.

photo by Patrick O'Connor • February 1986 in *Worcester Magazine*

GTE workers having coffee in the first-floor, well-windowed cafeteria thirty feet farther up the hill couldn't miss the stunning sight of blood on the sign and in new fallen snow.

While our previous demonstrations used a religious approach, sometimes ecumenical and sometimes specifically Catholic, the current action took place on a secular holiday devoted to a universal value. By using the shocking symbol of blood alongside a giant Valentine's Day message, we hoped to reach a broader audience.

Our leaflet, entitled "Love Disarms," read:

We have come to GTE this Valentine's Day to proclaim Love; not the love which shows itself in flowers, cards, and candy for those who routinely love us back, but the love that accepts risk out of concern and caring. We pour our blood to make clear the human cost of the nuclear and conventional weapons work done here.

In GTE literature, we read terms like 'Peacekeeper,' 'Strategic Defense Initiative,' and 'Command, Control, and Communications System.' There are no photos of Hiroshima and Nagasaki victims, no mention of the indiscriminate slaughter the computers are programmed to execute, nowhere are the world's starving millions depicted alongside the multi-billion-dollar GTE contracts. Our blood serves as a stark reminder that neither deceptive language nor high technology can cloak the reality that the work done here is the work of Death.

We hold our banner with a faith and firm belief that there is a way out of a psychology and economy that is continuing to grow more and more dependent on the military. It is with the spirit of a love that calls for trust and disarmament that we pour out our own blood in hope to save lives.

Patrick O'Connor, a free-lance photographer, and several reporters pulled up moments after we raised our banner.

I was later quoted in *Worcester Magazine* saying, "The blood on the GTE sign is just a case of honesty in advertising." *The Evening Gazette*, *The Voice*, *The Middlesex News*, and *Worcester Telegram* all ran stories with photos.

Carol and I were arrested and charged with trespassing and malicious destruction of property under a hundred dollars. At our arraignment, we pleaded not guilty and were released on personal recognizance until trial on March 5.

Out of fear that damaging the sign could result in my being sent to jail for a half a year, I stood by while Carol splattered the sign with blood from both of us. As it turned out, the police charged us identically.

We decided in advance of trial not to mount an elaborate necessity or international law defense, but rather just to make simple statements of

GTE employee cleans blood from his company's sign.

photo by Ben Mazur • February 20, 1986 in *The Voice*

our motivations and accept the consequences. When we and our supporters entered the Westborough District Court, I was surprised to see that our prosecutor was Harold Johnson, the DA who had prosecuted us at the jury trial in Worcester.

Evidently, he had taken considerable ribbing from other lawyers that it took him three days to win a conviction over pro-se peaceniks. When I said, "Good morning, Mr. Johnson" and waved, he just glared at me. When Judge Paul LoConto, someone we hadn't faced before, opened the proceeding, Mr. Johnson made a motion to disallow the necessity defense, something the judge set aside when Carol and I said we had no intention of presenting it.

The case for the Commonwealth went as usual: a GTE witness and two Westborough police officers testifying about what we did and our refusal to leave, things we did not dispute.

Carol began her testimony by describing her three-year-long peace walk. Unlike everyone else in the courtroom, Carol knew children, women, and men in the Soviet Union who would be killed in a nuclear war waged by the United States with weapons made at GTE.

The Worcester Telegram quoted her as saying,

> I chose blood because it is a visually articulate symbol. I wanted to call out to the hearts of GTE workers that day and appeal to their consciences. I cannot acknowledge the charge of trespassing because I consider GTE property the sacred earth of Native Americans, land that was stolen from Native Americans.

She went on to testify, "The work done by GTE workers is maliciously destructive." I testified

> I am a Roman Catholic struggling to be a good Christian. I was at GTE to proclaim that love calls us to disarmament. The work done at GTE could potentially incinerate everyone in this courtroom.

Scott Schaeffer-Duffy and Carol Bellin wait in the Westborough District Court lobby on March 5, 1986, for trial to begin for their presence in February at GTE
photo by John McDonnell in March 6, 1986 *Middlesex News*

The DA cross-examined each of us closely as to the identity of the doctor who drew our blood, but I said it was irrelevant to the case, and the judge agreed.

After the brief trial concluded with guilty findings on both charges, Judge LoConto asked what the state recommended. Citing my previous convictions, the DA asked for the maximum jail sentence, thirty days on the first charge and sixty on the second. He proposed forty-five days' jail time for Carol despite it being her first arrest at GTE.

Then Judge LoConto said to Carol and me, "I don't suppose you'd agree to pay a fine."

"We cannot in good conscience," I replied.

"And you won't agree to probation either?" he said.

When we shook our heads in the negative, he asked, "How about community service?"

"What we did at GTE was community service," Carol offered.

A bit exasperated, the judge asked, "So, what sentence would the defense recommend?"

Shooting from the hip, I said, "A guilty finding with no sentence."

After sighing audibly, Judge LoConto said, "I'm going to need a recess to think this over."

We all stood as he left the courtroom and braced ourselves for a too familiar Pontius Pilate scene when the judge washes his hands of responsibility for sending us to jail.

We figured our moral and political scruples would bring out a standard "my-hands-are-tied"/"you-have-sent-yourselves-to-jail" speech.

In light of all my public criticism of Worcester County Jail, I braced myself for three months' incarceration on my own under the thumb of potentially bitter guards.

What we imagined as our last minutes in civilian clothes with friends passed all too quickly before Judge LoConto reappeared and banged the gavel for order. He looked us both in the eye and said, "In the matter of the Commonwealth of Massachusetts vs. Carol Bellin and Scott Schaeffer-Duffy, I order a guilty finding to be put on file. You are free to go."

The courtroom erupted in cheers and tears. Absolutely flabbergasted, I hugged Carol and noticed over her shoulder how angry Harold Johnson looked. I kind of felt bad for him while simultaneously thinking, "Maybe, just maybe, over time, we might actually win this campaign against the MX at GTE."

When *The Middlesex News* asked how I felt about the sentence, I said, "I'm very pleased. But it doesn't mean that I won't go back to GTE and protest again."

Fourteen years later, I took up long distance running. Since then, I've finished fourteen marathons. I know intimately that well-meaning spectator shouts of "You're almost there" are not remotely true until the finish line is in sight.

On March 6 and April 1, 1986, Clark University graduate students Sam Thomas and Matt Sakkas completed two community studies of GTE in Westborough, opening yet another front in opposition to work on the MX missile.

On Friday, August 8, at the regular weekly vigil, we held banners reading, "Pray for Disarmament," "Peace Begins in the Heart," and "Bread not Bombs," the latter featuring a woodcut by Tom Lewis.

Nellie LeBeau, Ernie LeBeau's teenage daughter, appeared with a big smile behind a banner reading "Swords Into Plowshares" in a *Middlesex News* photo. Headlined, "10 Remember Nagasaki in Mild Protest at GTE," the article said the protesters gave out copies of the *Catholic Radical*, the newsletter for the then proposed Saints Francis and Thérèse Catholic Worker house of hospitality for the homeless which Dan Ethier, Claire, and I worked to found.

When asked why we did not commit civil disobedience until we got the shelter going, Claire said it would be "unproductive to get thrown in jail."

When the reporter asked why I kept coming back to protest, I said, "I never get frustrated, because what we are doing has to do with the life, death, and resurrection of Jesus. The truth of non-violence has already been proven by Jesus."

Solitary Witness

While the overwhelming number of our efforts to convert GTE were legal, civil disobedience remained part of our campaign. Dan Ethier, of the previous year's thirty-nine days in jail Hell, stepped up to the plate next.

In the second edition of *The Catholic Radical*, which came out in late September, Dan wrote an article entitled, "Risking Arrest at GTE" where he said:

> On October 1, I will try to walk into the GTE building in Westborough carrying a placard with the face of the crucified Christ and the words, "Love as I have." (John 15:12) Disarm.
>
> I will do this because GTE in Westborough is the GTE Strategic Systems division, where they work on the system that will allow the United States to fight a nuclear war long after all of us are dead.
>
> My hope is that the face of the crucified Christ, who told us to love our enemies and pray for those who persecute us, will inspire the people who work at GTE to follow his example of suffering love and disarm.
>
> Of course, this is illegal. But in Mark 3:1-6, we read that as Jesus was about to heal someone on the Sabbath, which was also illegal, he asked those who were offended, "Is it against the law to do good or evil, to save life or destroy it?" Then he healed the man, breaking the law.
>
> So, is it against the law to do good or to save lives? The work that GTE does threatens to kill us all. I believe that, if we would follow the example of Jesus, we must go to places like GTE and tell the workers this truth, even though many will be offended.

ink on paper by Dan Ethier • August 10, 1986 in *Catholic Free Press*

In the leaflet, he distributed at GTE he described himself as "a community member of the Saints Francis & Thérèse Catholic Worker who came to GTE during the week when we celebrate the feasts of these two saints." Thérèse of Lisieux and Francis of Assisi are commemorated on October 1 and 4, respectively.

That morning, Dan got dropped off at the main entrance and walked right past security to a room filled with desks of engineers separated by movable barriers, a work environment Dan knew well from his time working at Data General. For about twenty minutes, he passed out leaflets to a dozen workers, talked to some about his opposition to making nuclear weapons, and, when asked to leave, knelt down.

According to *The Catholic Free Press*, when one worker told him, he had "no right to disturb their work," Dan said, "Because your work creates victims, I do have a right to disturb it."

He went on to tell the *Free Press*, "I understand that many of them were people doing a job to support their families. Yet, at the same time, I wanted to nag their consciences."

Eventually GTE security and Westborough Police arrived, and an officer asked Dan, "Are you going to be a gentleman about this?" before peacefully escorting him to a waiting cruiser.

Meanwhile, six of us standing on GTE property held a banner with the same message as Dan's sign, "Love as I have, Disarm."

After Dan's arrest and a warning to those of us on the property that if we did not leave, we would be arrested too, we withdrew without incident.

Interestingly, in that night's edition of the *Evening Gazette*, Dan's arresting officer, Paul S. Donnelly, said,

Officer Paul Donnelly escorts Dan Ethier into Westborough District Court.

photo by John McDonnell in October 2, 1986 *Middlesex News*

> All the GTE people call the protesters by their first name. They're very nice people. They're not violent. They're not rude—or any other of the things that you associate with people who are usually arrested.

At his arraignment before Judge Stanford Strogoff, Dan pled not guilty to trespass and was released on personal recognizance until November 19.

After asking Dan to promise to return for trial, Judge Strogoff inquired, "Did you ever hear the expression, 'If you dance, you have to pay the piper?'"

"I've heard that," Dan replied.

With firmness, the judge went on to ask, "Do you know what that means?"

The proceedings ended when Dan said, "I do, your honor."

Would that testy character be Dan's trial judge? No one knew.

When asked by the *Gazette* whether he preferred Judge Brewin or Judge Strogoff for trial, Dan said he was prepared to go to jail, but "I'd prefer to go home."

In the wild, unpredictable ride that made up our Witness for Peace at GTE, neither judge heard Dan's case. An elderly judge named Stanley Joblonski sat on the bench in a small, side-room court in Westborough. As I waited for Dan's case to begin, I noticed how Judge Joblonski went to great pain to interview each convicted person and to tailor their punishment in creative and constructive ways. In six instances, he never sent anyone to jail. He seemed like a defense attorney's dream and prosecutor's nightmare.

After the prosecution presented their standard case, Judge Joblonski asked GTE chief of security Michael Augustine what GTE does at the plant. "Do they make telephones there?"

Mr. Augustine replied, "No, we're mainly in the military business."

Dan took the stand to tell what he had done at GTE and why. After he finished, Judge Joblonski peppered him with personal questions about where he lived, worked, and went to school. He showed particular interest in Dan's thesis for a master's degree in religious studies at Assumption College.

Before rendering a verdict, the judge asked the prosecutor what sentence he would recommend if Dan was convicted. The DA said, "Fourteen days in jail."

"He won't pay fines. He won't accept probation," the prosecutor went on with a shrug. "I'm at a loss what else to suggest."

Following him, the probation officer opposed giving Dan community service saying, "These actions have to stop, and community service won't do that."

Then the judge asked Dan when he planned to finish his thesis, to which Dan replied, "I told my advisor I'd finish by May."

The judge then continued the case until May 1, to be dismissed if the thesis is turned in to the court by that date.

"I just want to help you finish your thesis," the remarkable Judge Joblonski concluded.

True to his word, Dan finished by the required date.

Could there possibly be any other surprises in store?

More Lovers

Tom Lewis introduced Claire, me, and many others to a collection of spiritually-based antiwar activists who twice a year held a retreat to confer, socialize, pray, and plan future protests. The group calls itself the Atlantic Life Community, ALC. Through it, we came to know seasoned activists as well as newcomers. Many members lived in communities including Catholic Worker houses. Quite a few were married with children, as Claire and I are. The gatherings offered a wonderful balance of joy and challenge.

At the Labor Day 1986 ALC retreat in Bangor, Pennsylvania, the group decided to offer its support to the Peace Witness at GTE by joining us on Valentine's Day 1987. Because ALC members were scattered all over the east coast of the US, those willing to risk arrest wondered if there was a way to deal with legal consequences right away.

A police officer bars forward movement of Dan Lawrence, left, and Scott Schaeffer-Duffy during Valentine's Day 1987 Peace Witness at GTE.
photo by John McDonnell in February 14, 1987 *Middlesex News*

Tom told them that Judge Brewin had refused to accept our Good Friday 1985 offer to plead guilty. Brewin entered not guilty pleas on our behalf and set us free until trial more than a month later. ALC folks were willing to come up to Worcester and even stay for a thirty-day jail sentence, but did not want to drive there twice, so we decided to try something new. If we told the judge at arraignment we believed we had done nothing wrong and would, therefore, not return for trial, he—at that time all the judges we'd seen were men—would either try us on the spot or hold us in jail until trial. In the latter case, we'd likely be sentenced to time served. In theory, the tactic sounded good, but previous experience led us not to make any promises.

Up to then, except for the Walls of Jericho protest, most antiwar gatherings at GTE had modest participation, but the ALC bumped up our numbers. On February 14, 1987, seventy-five people from as far away as Toronto and Baltimore gathered across the road from GTE. Claire welcomed everyone on behalf of Saints Francis and Thérèse Catholic

Worker. Musicians led us in a beautiful song: "Love, love, Love, love. People, we are made for love. Love each other as ourselves for we are all one."

Westborough police arrest Dan Lawrence, Deidre Nuñez, and Clare Grady, from left, at GTE on February 14, 1987.
photo by John McDonnell in February 14, 1987 *Middlesex News*

John Pendleton from Boston read the following poem by the Jesuit priest, Dan Berrigan.

> Sometime in your life,
> hope that you might see
> one starved person—
> the look on their face
> when the bread finally arrives.
> Hope that you might have baked it
> or bought it or even kneaded it yourself.
>
> For that look on their face,
> for your hand touching theirs
> across a piece of bread,
> you might be willing
> to lose a lot
> or suffer a lot
> or die a little
> even.

We followed the poem by breaking and sharing bread while singing in Latin "Ubi caritas et amor, ubi caritas deus ibi es."—"God is where charity and love are."

Led by nine of us willing to go directly to jail, most of the group crossed the road. Kathleen Rumpf from Ithaca, New York, told *Worcester Magazine* that I intended to walk to the GTE sign and again pour my own blood on it, but a line of police officers blocking the driveway prevented that from happening.

For fifteen minutes, police and demonstrators effectively prevented access to the plant. When it became clear that no protester would reach the GTE sign, I poured my blood in the snow beside the crowd.

In its margins, the leaflet prepared for the day featured artwork by Jackie Allen from Hartford highlighting a heart breaking a bomb in two. The leaflet said,

> On this Valentine's Day, we rededicate ourselves to love, the love that reconciles people to one another. True affection requires the instruments of hatred and death to fall from our hands.
>
> This blood is a call to conversion and to hope. On this Valentine's Day, we say, "Enough bloodshed. Love disarms."

Ultimately, police arrested me with Teri Allen of Hartford; Peter DeMott and George Ostensen of Baltimore; Clare Grady and Marian Mollin of Ithaca; Deirdre Nuñez and Dan Lawrence from Worcester; and Kimberly Crawford, an eighteen-year-old student at Worcester's Clark University.

Police whisked us to the Westborough police station, held us briefly in cells, processed us, and brought us to court for arraignment.

Called first by Judge Matthew McCann, I stood and approached the bench as requested. My eighteen-month-old son Justin jumped out of Claire's arms and ran to me calling "Daddy, Daddy," until Claire scooped him up.

I apologized to the judge and told him, "He thought I was going to jail." I then tried to contextualize our refusal to promise to appear and convince the judge to deal with us immediately. I said, "All of us are not from the area, and it would be a hardship to come back for trial."

Nonetheless, Judge McCann entered not guilty pleas on our behalf, set trial for April 17, which happened to be Good Friday, and released us without bail. He explained, "We do not arrest people because they might break the law. We arrest people when they do break the law."

If we didn't show up for trial, he said, the court would issue warrants for our arrest, but not until we failed to appear. A statement that we had no intention of appearing meant nothing to the court.

While the oldest member of our group, the recidivist Dan Lawrence, had just turned fifty-four, the novice, Kimberly Crawford, remained a teenager. She had convinced the rest of us that she had the maturity to risk arrest at GTE because she had been arrested once before, on December 16, 1986, for protesting the launch of the eleventh Trident submarine in Groton, Connecticut. She could have had that case dismissed by paying a sixty-eight-dollar fine at her arraignment but refused and joined six others asking for a trial set for March 1987.

In the 1980s, it wasn't uncommon for peace activists to have two or more cases pending at the same time. The threat of nuclear war loomed so large that John Pendleton once told me, "Be in jail or die of shame."

Some activists refused to participate in what they called civil disobedience as theater. At many large protests, police arrested people, sat them down on the sideline, and left them unattended and unrestrained while arresting others. Hard core protesters got right back up and returned to the blockade or whatever other form of protest. Unless officers locked them in transport vehicles, those folks returned over and over. You can well imagine how angry that made the police, but it underscored that there was nothing symbolic about their protest.

At a national demonstration against the Trident submarine in King's Bay, Georgia, the east coast base for the subs, a conflict arose between the base and the King's Bay Police Department as to who should have jurisdiction at entrance of the naval base. The locals argued that the expense of the large protest should be borne by the military police who had lots of federal dollars, but the base commander washed his hands of the whole thing.

The arrangement angered the supervising King's Bay sheriff so much that he allowed police officers to take demonstrators away thirty at a time in waiting buses, drive them around the corner, and set them free with assurances that no one would stop anyone from returning to the gates and blockading again. In that way, the sheriff transformed a protest that might have lasted an hour into one that blocked the base's main gate most of the day. I think, I was arrested three times that day without being charged even once.

In a February 26, 1987 interview in the Clark University student newspaper the *Scarlet*, Kimberly said she understood that the protest at GTE could land her in jail for thirty days but that,

> In 1985, there were approximately eighteen thousand megatons of nuclear weapons in the world. It would only take three hundred megatons to destroy all the large and medium cities. That would end civilization as we know it.

With considerable wisdom, she went on,

> I think a lot of people around Clark are very unsure how to feel. I think there's a tendency to not do anything. People need to be educated and to take a stand on these issues. People have to realize that nuclear war is possible, and we have to do everything we can to stop it.

If sentenced to jail at the April 17 trial, she mused that the judge might grant a stay until she finished the spring semester but recognized: "An important thing is sticking together, so if everyone goes to jail, I probably will too."

On Holy Thursday, April 16, the day before our trial, eight people were arrested for protesting at GTE. Repeat offenders Tom Lewis and Daniel Sicken were joined by newcomers, all from Massachusetts, Sarah Jeglosky of Worcester's newly founded Saints Francis and Thérèse Catholic Worker; Meg Brodhead, a reporter for the *Catholic Free Press;* Wayne Petrin of Ware, Jonnie Lieberman of Boston, Alice Kidder of Berlin, and Jamie Babson of Shutesbury. They were arraigned on the morning of April 17 and released until trial in July.

As it turned out, everyone except for Peter DeMott returned for our trial resulting from our Valentine's Day action. Peter wrote a letter notifying the court that he would be protesting at the Pentagon on April 17. He had no fear of a misdemeanor warrant three states away from his home.

In preparation for our trial later that day, I warned my new co-defendants that, if we faced Judge Brewin, he would be very restrictive about what we could say on the stand.

Lo and behold, our old adversary did hear our case. After the prosecution presented the usual evidence, George Ostensen was called as the first witness for the defense. With his long hair neatly tied behind his head in a ponytail, George walked up to the stand carrying a Bible. After swearing to tell the truth and only the truth, he told Judge Brewin that he had gone to GTE largely in response to a biblical text that he wanted to read, but as soon as he opened his Bible, Brewin banged his gavel and said he would not allow the reading. George replied that it was very short, but that made no difference.

"The Bible is not relevant to today's charges," the judge replied.

Undeterred, George began to read, only to have the furious judge drown out his words.

A bit shell-shocked, George waved his arms and said, "It will only take a minute."

Brewin then threatened to hold George in contempt, a move that prompted George to gesture so dramatically that his hair came untied and flew out in all directions.

At Brewin's order, a court officer forcibly escorted George off the stand while he continued shouting almost hysterically, "I just want to read from the Bible!"

I looked over to Dan Lawrence and said, "Looks like we're all going to have to be exceptionally calm after that."

Aside from descriptions of our physical actions at GTE, each of us could only squeeze in the tiniest hints of our motivation. For example, my entire testimony was something like, "I crossed Research Drive onto GTE property carrying a sign saying Love Disarms. When stopped by Westborough police officers, I knelt down and prayed for nuclear disarmament until I was arrested."

In short order, we were all found guilty. Not surprisingly, George, Dan Lawrence, and I got the maximum sentence, 30 days, plus five extra for refusing to pay $15 in court costs. The other five defendants refused to pay $62.50 in fines and fees and were sent to jail for 25 days.

On April Fools Day, twenty-one days before the jail sentence, the Saints Francis and Thérèse Catholic Worker house on Jaques Avenue in Worcester burned down in a fire. Dan Ethier, Sarah Jeglosky, Kenny Stewart, Ron Hesselton, Joe Devoe, Scott and Claire Schaeffer-Duffy, and their young son Justin had lived there.

The jail sentence compounded difficulties of being homeless. One never knows when one risks arrest what curve balls life can throw by the time a trial concludes.

After Scott's release from jail, he and his family found shelter with the Little Franciscans of Mary until purchase of the house at 52 Mason Street, Worcester, where Scott and Claire live as members of the Catholic Worker movement.

An April 22, 1987, *Worcester Magazine* article entitled, "The Familiar Melody of Protest," concluded:

> Many of those protesting against GTE have ties with the Catholic Church and have been arrested before. Teri Allen, a registered nurse from Hartford, has worked at Jesuit Volunteer Corps projects in North Philadelphia, southeast Kentucky, and in Thailand. She said that returning to the United States, after spending time in Third World countries, she was struck by the level of affluence in the United States. She said,
>
>> People in the developing world told me that their problems were rooted in our country. We have military bases everywhere. These are the real victims of the nuclear arms race.
>
> She said,
>
>> We're not crazy. This isn't a fad. The media should focus on the weapons, not on us. We don't want to be celebrities.

On April 21, with Dan, George, and eight other inmates also signing, I wrote a letter to the *Worcester Telegram* about adverse jail conditions. Emboldened by extensive previous press coverage, I included a cover letter asking the T*elegram* to

> Please accept this letter even though it is not typed. Most forms of redress for grievances are cut off to us here and you would be doing us a service to print our letter.

Here's the letter I wrote:

Dear Editor,

In spite of consent degrees, laws, regulations, and a forty-page exposé on abusive conditions at the Worcester County Jail, the mistreatment of inmates goes on. Here in maximum security, men are crowded into cells built for one. Half of us get a bunk while the other half sleep on the floor by the toilet. An entire tier of men (more than forty) has been locked down for five days now because a couple of them committed an infraction. Jail procedure allows such a lockup for only twenty-four hours after an incident during which time a deputy is supposed to conduct an investigation. But that's not so here—the guards lock everyone up, denying them visits, exercise, phone calls, showers, and even Easter Sunday religious services in order to create enough pressure for someone to confess to the infraction. The men, almost all of them completely innocent of wrongdoing, have begun yelling and rattling the bars on their cells. Soon the guards will charge more of them with infractions even though they are being provoked. No jail officials seem to care that rights are being denied and violence instigated.

On our tier, men classified for minimum security are being denied contact visits. For weeks, some of them have been able to see wives and children only through thick Plexiglas while a contact visit room lies only a few feet away.

We are vulnerable to lockups at any time. Several men are locked up now for bringing fruit back from breakfast. (We can buy food to eat in our cells but cannot bring food from the cafeteria. Whatever we don't eat in our ten- or fifteen-minute mealtime has to be thrown away). We can be locked up for oversleeping, standing in the hall by the phone, taking too long to eat, and, more significantly considering our mistreatment, for writing a petition, holding a group meeting, organizing a nonviolent protest, or refusing any guard's order no matter how unjust or ridiculous. We can be locked up and cut off from outside contact at any time, even as in a group lockup if we haven't done anything wrong.

The jail world is a private one kept from public scrutiny by distance, fences, snow-white walls, and the complete failure of the government to defend inmates' rights. This jail—in fact, all jails—need regular visits by citizens' watchdog groups which will tour the jail and hear the grievances of the prisoners. We rely on outside concern. Even this letter could cause each of us serious mistreatment. One inmate was denied a furlough in 1983, according to a deputy, because of "negative comments in the newspapers." Please don't turn your backs. Demand changes at the jail."

Once again, I hoped a creative intervention could help prevent a riot, and, once again, I failed.

A week later, Robert Foster of the *Telegram* editorial board replied, "Dear Mr. Duffy, I'm sorry to have to tell you that it is our policy not to publish letters concerning prison conditions written by current inmates."

He returned my letter. All incoming mail is opened by jail authorities, so instead of improving conditions, the letter bought all of us who signed it three days in lockup.

That setback didn't mean the media forgot us. On May 9, the *Catholic Free Press* ran an article entitled, "Convicted on Good Friday: Witness continues behind bars for war resisters in County Jail."

That article cites George Ostensen's words:

> The same machine that perpetrates the militaristic lie has forced the poor into this jail for ridiculous things. The purpose of the arms race is to keep people at the bottom of the pile. Some of these men have turned to drugs, alcohol, or "rip-offs" as they've lost hope of getting out of oppression. Many have committed only minor offenses because they don't have all the benefits wealthier people have. We live in a culture that is not providing life or love. Our society is built on false gods and possessed by the demon of death. Americans have put their faith and security in the powers of death. As Christians, we're called upon to confront those powers.

On the other hand, Dan Lawrence described his fifth jail sentence as the "easiest, quietest, and most restful." He attributed his "inner peacefulness" in part to sharing a cell with me, a person he described as "afraid of no one." He added, "I feel a camaraderie of brotherliness and concern among the men for each other" in spite of "human rights violations" and "very undesirable conditions."

Borrowing a phrase I heard from Phil Berrigan, I told the *Free Press* that jail is "the new monastery." I said, "Suddenly, I have to be inactive. It's a time when I am trying to trust that I don't have to be out doing everything myself and that God will use me here in a fruitful way."

While saying that being in jail for an act of conscience can be liberating, I recognized how inmates not incarcerated by choice, "can be deeply hurt by the experience."

The article noted that our co-defendants, Deirdre Nuñez and Kimberly Crawford after a week in jail in MCI Framingham, paid the balance of their fines so they could be released. Clare Grady, Marian Mollin, and Teri Allen served the entire twenty-five-day sentence.

Teri had a letter entitled "Jail ministry from the inside" in the same issue of the *Free Press* that ran the article about us. It read:

To the Editor:

When I come into jail, I receive the experience the same way I did going to Thailand with Maryknoll. It's a new culture, language, and reality, and I need to learn a lot to survive in order to do the work I was called to do here.

The way I do that is to stay as centered as I possibly can—and pay attention—keep my eyes and heart open. I am not the savior here (even though I believe in doing jail ministry from the inside). I have a lot of empowering to do. People come to you looking for a centered person, someone who will listen. But as in all our work, we cannot give from our surplus. So, we have a responsibility to do what we need to do to keep centered, to keep our wells full (meditate, pray, read Scripture, whatever), and as in any place or situation when we go to serve, we receive so much more than we can possibly give.

Something that I have seen that attracts negative responses from other jailed women is peace activists acting or requesting that they be treated differently by constantly giving anti-nuclear raps or saying things about the "lesbians in here" or saying things like "but we are the protesters."

It is my firm belief that no one should be in this human warehouse. It is wild to watch the dynamics here, the power plays between inmates and guards, the screaming guards do to people on the edge, power trips, talking to people like they have no dignity and value. And then, the women to the women—threats, old inmates (I hate that word) harassing the new ones, people just watching out for who looks weak and wham—you're marked. It's so clear to see the spiral of violence spin on, be fueled, nurtured, ingrained in most dynamics, and actually gain momentum.

It strikes me as odd that Judge Brewin sent us here as punishment, here among the disempowered. It's so easy to see that we must begin to develop creative non-violent alternatives so we can survive. We must be about true Christian/feminist relationships that empower everyone involved. Helping people touch again the power deep within them—their ability to gain greater understanding through their anger rather than being slaves to it. We don't share and empower through raps. It's through how we relate and interact, by refusing to get sucked away by the dynamic—that perhaps is the hardest part.

We all bring our giftedness, our blessedness, our beauty into every situation and environment we move into. We also bring our baggage—our issues, our brokenness, our deep need for healing. It's always with us, as is our responsibility to embrace that healing and live as faithful people whether we are in our homes, with our families, or locked away for twenty-two hours a day with three other women. Jail or going overseas sounds rather dramatic, but it's still you living every day as a child of God. I guess that's a challenge, no matter where.

Just so you don't think we were a bunch of goody two-shoes, I must confess that George and I got into numerous arguments over how best to live Christian simplicity. One day, while we were bickering in my cell, I heard another inmate comment, "The peace activists are fighting again."

The Last Civil Disobedience

After stacking two acts of civil disobedience on top of each other, no one risked arrest for two years. I don't remember why.

The weekly vigil continued, but GTE's work on the MX did as well. Shortly after the Holy Thursday arrests in 1987, GTE Public Affairs Manager Claire Deveney said that President Reagan's proposal to deploy fifty MX missiles "certainly could mean hundreds of millions of dollars."

In a March 1988 television interview about the Strategic Defense Initiative nicknamed Star Wars, Richard Fidler, GTE vice president and general manager of the Westborough plant, admitted that most GTE engineers did not believe that Star Wars would work but, on the chance that it might, five to ten years of research would be done.

Seven years of leaflets, letters, shareholder activism, vigils, fasts, marches, trials, and jail sentences had not slowed the GTE military juggernaut. On the contrary, GTE seemed smugly sure of itself that many more millions of dollars would come their way from the Pentagon.

While "The definition of insanity is doing the same thing over and over again

1987 Holy Thursday defendants for witness at GTE created an invitation to their jury trial.
permanent marker on paper by Scott Schaeffer-Duffy

and expecting different results," according to an anonymous quote often attributed to Albert Einstein, we soldiered on with another act of civil disobedience.

On August 7, 1989, the day after the forty-fourth anniversary of the atomic bombing of Hiroshima, after attending mass celebrated at Saint Luke's Church by Bishop George Rueger, Hattie Nestel of New England Peace Pagoda in Leverett; Ken Synan of Levittown, New York; Tom Lewis, and Jenifer Hoffman and I from the Saints Francis and Thérèse Catholic Worker carried photos of Soviet citizens onto GTE property. The leaflet we distributed explained,

> Although no warheads are assembled in Westborough, the ability of the Pentagon to rain nuclear devastation on very specific Soviet targets depends on places like GTE. We are carrying photographs of Soviet children, women, and men to remind us that the US is still ready to incinerate them in less than eight minutes. Our common humanity is so very much more important than our political differences.

At noon, each of us was dropped off close to the GTE building. We walked across the lawn past the GTE sign to about six feet from the glass windows to the cafeteria. We knelt down, displaying the photos to workers we could see eating lunch. Although there was a door for them to come outside and sit at one of several picnic tables, no one did so.

Hattie started the Japanese Buddhist chant, "Na mu myoho renge kyo"—often translated as "These are the words the Buddha said" or "All life is sacred." Ken started singing. GTE security asked us to leave. We declined. Police came and asked us to leave. We declined again. They paused and then asked twice more. All the while, workers looked out. No one lost their temper or gestured negatively—not the workers, not the police, not security, and certainly not us.

We were arrested, processed, and then arraigned before District Court Judge Margaret Brennan, (the first woman judge we had seen). As we did once before, we opted to present a defense of necessity before a jury of our peers. Judge Brennan accepted our request to represent ourselves and set October 3 for our first hearing in Worcester Superior Court. Before the judge adjourned, Hattie offered her an origami peace crane, which the judge politely suggested be left on the court clerk's desk.

Hoffman, youngest member of the group and recently graduated from high school in Brooklyn, told the *Middlesex News* she was not afraid of going to jail. "The people in (apartheid) South Africa and the (Israeli-occupied) West Bank are going through much worse. This is a chance to be in solidarity with other peace activists."

We were excited to go on trial in Worcester's stately courthouse built in 1845 and overlooking Main Street. Unfortunately, our hearing on October 3 did not prove awe-inspiring.

While people entering from Main Street climbed marble stairs between high pillars and then passed a life-size reproduction of Michaelangelo's sculpture of Moses holding the Ten Commandments to reach a majestic courtroom lined with polished wood, we entered by a back door on Harvard Street, virtually at street level, into a very small and unimpressive mini courtroom where we faced Judge Austin Philbin. After the charges against us were read, he exhaled audibly, and said, "In college, I was an activist who always feared the day would come when I would represent the establishment against activists like I once was."

But then, he straightened his back and declared sternly,

But I want you to know from the outset, that I will conduct this case strictly by the rules, and, if you are convicted, I will not show partiality or mercy. I'm setting trial to begin on October 31, and I expect all parties to be ready to proceed on that day.

A mixed introduction to say the least. A jury trial on Halloween in front of a conflicted judge. Our ducks would have to be in a very tight row. Clearly, it was not an instance when showing up in costume would lighten the mood.

So, we prepared our most thorough brief in support of necessity. We recruited Paul Walker, PhD; Professor Michael True, PhD; Ted Conna, MD; Roman Catholic Sister Rena Mae Gagnon, and Buddhist Sister Clare Carter to testify. We met regularly to prepare and practice. We sent trial invitations to our supporters and the press.

In all likelihood, depending on how long the jury deliberated, the proceedings would begin on Halloween and end on All Saints Day, November 1. That would be a good omen, better than having the case conclude on November 2, All Soul's Day, when Catholics recall the dead. With Tom Lewis, Hattie, and my prior convictions, we could easily be spending Thanksgiving and even Christmas in jail if convicted. We were well aware that no Massachusetts jury had previously accepted the necessity defense for activists. The bookies did not give us good odds.

To complicate matters, Claire and I had had a second child, Grace. Tom had married Andrea Borbely, an artist who did the graphic for our trial invitation, and they had a daughter, Nora Marie. Although Jennifer grew up

Hattie Nestel, Jennifer Hoffman, Ken Synan, Tom Lewis, and Scott Schaeffer-Duffy, from left, await Judge Austin Philbin in Worcester District Court.

photo courtesy of Scott Schaeffer-Duffy

in a Catholic Worker activist family, she was still only eighteen. Jewish Hattie lived with a dedicated Buddhist community. Ken was poetic in all senses of the word. Two of us had young children, one of us was very young, and the two others couldn't have been more different.

Hattie, for example, had a reputation for uncompromising principles. After being arrested previously with her and thirty others on Martin Luther King Day for protesting the Trident submarine in Groton, Connecticut, seven demonstrators decided to use King's name. The arraignment judge refused to take any of us out of the crowded holding cells who wouldn't give their real name.

After a couple of hours, a court officer came down and announced, "This is your last chance to be arraigned today. Step forward if you're willing to give your name. Those who don't will be taken to county jail until they do." A couple of University of Massachusetts students who participated in the demonstration after assurances that they'd be released the same day, stepped forward.

Hattie said, "Anyone who leaves these cells puts a knife in the back of solidarity."

Tom Lewis depicted the homeless in pen and ink drawings.
photo by Christopher Navin in June 1990 *Inside Worcester*

The students paled and froze in place. Feeling bad for them and also not wanting to go to jail to protect people's right to give a symbolic alias, I said, "Lighten up, Hattie" and walked out, giving others some cover to do the same. Hattie and several others stayed.

As a side note, the group that insisted on using King's name was brought back and forth to court from jail several times with none of them backing down and giving their own name. Civil rights leader Ralph Abernathy advocated for them to no avail. Finally, when the group had exceeded the maximum sentence of 30 days for their charge, the judge brought them in and said, "For crying out loud, none of you are even Black" and then released them all.

Tom Lewis was one of those Martin Luther Kings.

Ken, in stark contrast to Hattie, was a laid back, stop-and-smell-the-roses kind of guy. Tom and Andrea asked Ken to sing a psalm at their wedding. When Ken stood up to do so, he announced that he had to "tune up," so he spent the next five minutes stretching his throat, humming, saying "Me, me, me" and "La, la, la" and making other sounds before singing the psalm. Claire, who stood next to me on the altar, nearly burst out laughing.

Forget wondering if we could win a legal victory. Objective observers might wonder if our group could hold it together until the trial's completion.

The trial began at 9 a.m. on Halloween in a tiny courtroom where Judge Philbin heard our motion for necessity and Assistant District Attorney William F. George's rebuttal. After I said that civil disobedience was our last resort to avert nuclear war, George said our motives and any reference to nuclear weapons were irrelevant. After listening to both sides and reading our brief, the judge ruled in our favor.

So far, so good.

Then, Judge Philbin moved the proceedings to a bigger courtroom, where he instructed our supporters to leave the first three rows open for prospective jurors. After thirty women and men were escorted into those seats, he welcomed them and asked the standard questions that could excuse them. "Do you know any of the parties?" "Are you familiar with the case and have you already formed an opinion as to the defendants' guilt or innocence?"

He then told us and the prosecution that candidates would be brought up to the stand one at a time, and we could ask them questions. If we objected to a person being added to the jury, we could use up to six peremptory strikes to remove one without explanation. When those challenges were exhausted, a juror could only be excused for cause accepted by the judge.

The process moved along fairly quickly. In short order, eleven people were excused and six women seated in the jury box when the potential final juror came forward: a serious-looking middle-aged man with a very short haircut, who worked as a Massachusetts state trooper. Since law enforcement personnel generally took a dim view of civil disobedience, Hattie felt that he'd be predisposed against us, but we had already used up all our strikes. His occupation and demeanor did not convince the judge that he could not render a fair verdict. But all was not lost, since only five of the six jurors would actually deliberate. At the end of the trial, one of them would be randomly designated as an alternate and then excused. That made a fourteen-percent chance we'd lose the state trooper, but it was something.

The judge seated the jury, and the prosecutor wrapped up his case after calling the head of GTE security and a Westborough police officer.

When we did not contest any of their testimony, the prosecution rested.

We called our witnesses and laid the ground for a necessity defense. Paul Walker's credentials and expertise made his testimony about the danger of GTE's work on the MX vivid and terrifying. Ted Conn, a member of Physicians for Social Responsibility, spelled out the harmful psychological effect of the arms race on children. Michael True detailed the historical effectiveness of civil disobedience as a response to social injustice.

The prosecutor did not cross examine any of them. Sister Rena Mae Gagnon of the Little Franciscans of Mary described how the Catholic Church condemned the nuclear arms race in general and first-strike nuclear weapons. Sister Clare from the Peace Pagoda detailed how her order's founder came to oppose nuclear arms after witnessing the horrible devastation of Hiroshima.

Hattie Nestel, Michel Cahill, and Jennifer Hoffman, from left, wait for the jury verdict at the Harvard Street entrance to Worcester District Court.

photo courtesy of Scott Schaeffer-Duffy

Then, each of us took the stand in our own defense. Our diversity kept each testimony fresh. Everyone came across as sincere and serious. In a letter from all five of us that ran on November 15 in *Worcester Magazine*, we summarized our testimonies:

> Each of us brought something unique. Tom Lewis displayed his portraits of the homeless and touched on his work for peace which stretches back to Civil Rights days. Hattie Nestel, mother and woodsman, spoke movingly of how her Jewish consciousness of the Nazi Holocaust came to relate to the nuclear arms race. Ken Synan, parent and Central American sanctuary worker, read beautiful poetry. Jennifer Hoffman, a member of the Saints Francis and Thérèse Catholic Worker, spoke of her ten years living and working with the poor. And Scott Schaeffer-Duffy, husband to peace activist Claire and a Catholic Worker, shared his four-year-old son's painting which is titled "Peace for Children and Grownups."

When we finished, the DA asked each of us only two questions, "Did you hear GTE security and Westborough Police say you would be arrested for trespassing if you did not leave the property?" and "Did you comply with their requests and leave GTE property?"

After Tom, Jennifer, Hattie, and I, in turn, answered the first question "Yes" and the second one "No," George said, "No further questions."

But when Ken was asked if he heard the warning from security and police, he shocked everyone by answering, "No." Since I had knelt at GTE only a few feet from him and clearly heard the warnings, I didn't know what to make of Ken's reply.

Taken aback, the prosecutor said, "Security and police testified that they stood close to you all and warned you multiple times. Are you saying you did not hear them at all?"

Scott Schaeffer-Duffy, left, and Ken Synan reflect on Ken's explanation to the court about spirtual centering

photo courtesy of Scott Schaeffer-Duffy

Ken calmly answered, "They may have said something to me, but I was so spiritually centered that I was in a space where outside distractions could not break my inner calm."

The prosecutor looked confused, the jury laughed, and then even the judge said with a grin, "I guess it's an existential question."

Bruised but not defeated, George sat down, and the defense rested.

Judge Philbin said he would adjourn until the next day when he'd charge the jury and allow closing arguments.

To prepare ourselves, we held a meeting at the Saints Francis and Thérèse Catholic Worker house. All of us expected from past experience to be convicted, probably before midafternoon the next day.

In that event, Hattie proposed that we present a united front to Judge Philbin by refusing to accept probation or fines, leaving him only two choices, setting us free with no sentence as Judge LoConto did for Carol Bellin and me or sending us all to jail. With a "Which-side-are-you-on?" ferocity, we could demonstrate willingness to stand in solidarity with all the others who would be sent to jail that same day in Worcester.

We had taken the position before but never insisted that everyone toe the line. For different reasons, multiple people previously paid fines or accepted probation. Dan Ethier and I were released twenty-eight days early after the bishop paid the balance of our fines. Individual circumstances varied for every defendant.

That we would not all agree became clear when Tom attended the meeting with his wife, Andrea. I had always assumed that Tom, who had been arrested countless times and jailed for more than three years, would subscribe to Hattie's approach, but I didn't take into account how Tom's incarceration would leave Andrea and young Nora alone in a neighborhood awash in drug violence.

In fact, things had gotten so bad that, once a month, Tom invited various Catholic priests to come celebrate what he called "a street Mass" outside Tom's house. As with using Catholic symbols to promote disarmament, he believed a vested priest offering Mass at the corner of Austin and Piedmont streets could disarm the neighborhood. Though very possible, it had not come to pass yet. So, with Andrea's support, Tom said he'd be open to probation and a fine.

Of course, given Tom's record, those lesser sentences might not even be offered, but if they were, Tom wanted to be clear he'd accept them. Although the disagreement was sharp, we ended the meeting as congenially as we could and resolved to get some rest.

The next day, Judge Philbin excused one of the women alternate jurors after her name was pulled from a hat. The judge thanked her for her service. The state trooper remained. Not a good start, to say the least.

The judge then instructed the jury to reach a unanimous verdict and to remember that, if they wanted to acquit us on the basis of necessity, they must agree that we had exhausted *all* legal alternatives, that the harm we sought to abate was *undeniable*, and the means we chose to abate the harm were *effective*. His emphasis signaled doom.

For the next three hours, we hung around outside the courthouse until a court officer told us the jury had reached a verdict. The five of us were instructed to stand in the front row with the jury to our right and the judge just to our left. With white knuckles, Tom stood to my left clutching his sketchbook.

The judge asked, "Members of the jury, have you reached a verdict?"

The foreman, the state trooper, rose and said, "Yes, your honor."

The judge replied, "In the cases of the Commonwealth of Massachusetts against Jennifer Hoffman, Thomas Lewis, Harriet Nestel, Scott Schaeffer-Duffy, and Kenneth Synan, what say you all?"

You could have heard a pin drop in the few seconds it took him to reply, "Not guilty on all charges."

The courtroom erupted in cheers and hugs. The celebration was so loud I could barely hear the judge thanking the jury and announcing, "Case closed."

Amid the joyful chaos, I approached the bench to thank Judge Philbin, who told me,

> While I'm sure you're relieved, I have to confess I am, too. My girlfriend told me last night that, if I sent you all to jail, she'd break up with me, but I felt I had no other option. I hardly slept. I am so relieved not to have to face that choice.

As I walked away, I saw Ken generously offer his hand to the prosecutor, who, looked like he was in shock, and said, "YOU are the last person I want to talk to."

A few minutes later, still in shock, we gathered outside the courthouse in a circle to offer a prayer of gratitude. Just before we could begin, the state trooper tapped me on the shoulder and said, "I want you all to know that for two hours, I was the only juror who wanted to find you not guilty."

How's that for a miracle?

The press responded with enthusiasm. The *Middlesex News* headline on November 2, 1989, read, "5 GTE protesters cleared; Group claims first Victory." In front-page coverage, the *Worcester Telegram* featured a quote from me: "This helps lift our spirits. I think the jurors were very courageous."

With tears of joy streaming down her face, Hattie told the press, "Even though I do other things, I must do this."

Three weeks after our trial, the Soviet Union collapsed. Demand rose for dramatic cuts in military spending. The MX missile program was canceled. On March 3, 1991, the *Worcester Telegram & Gazette* announced, "GTE closing facility." The GTE Corporation went out of business nine years later.

What Did the Workers Think?

In retrospect, I wonder about the significance of our nine-year campaign against the MX missile at GTE in Westborough. Did our actions influence political and corporate leaders? Did we change the minds of any of GTE's workers?

In trying to ferret out the answer to the latter question, I'm reminded of an event from the mid 1980s when Michael Cahill and I joined a demonstration at the Pentagon. We held a banner made from a long sheet saying, "WAR Hurts Us All." Without blocking the entire way, we stood on a pedestrian bridge crowded with military and civilian workers going inside. After a few minutes, an angry man charged forward wielding the sharp point of an umbrella that ripped the sheet in two. Undeterred, I told Michael we could still hold the word WAR since it was in large block letters with red dripping off the sides to suggest bloodshed.

After about twenty minutes, a polite army officer approached us and said, "Excuse me, but just what does your sign mean?"

We looked down and realized that we were holding a banner that said WA.

We learned the lesson that it is very important for protesters to present something intelligible to those they hope to persuade.

In protests where people can stop and chat, it is relatively easy to test the effectiveness of one's protest. At a weekly peace vigil in Worcester's busy Lincoln Square where stopping vehicles is not safe, we often keep count of how many drivers give us the finger, a thumb's down, or other indication of opposition and how many show support by making a peace sign, waving, tooting their horn, or giving us a thumbs up. While fewer than one in ten passing drivers weigh in, it is some kind of barometer on our effectiveness. Interestingly, we noticed during the first Gulf War, when yellow support-the-troops ribbons abounded, the most vigorous pro-war drivers were white men between twenty and forty years old who drove pickup trucks. Not a single, eighteen-wheel truck driver ever opposed us.

Knowing whether or not one's methods are communicative is not only good politics, it's also a preventative measure against wasting time. No one wants to demonstrate week after week in all kinds of weather with incomprehensible or completely alienating signs. Only egomaniacs focus on washing their own hands of evil. Other-centered activists care about those they hope to win over, something that cannot be achieved without intelligence, patience, humility, compassion, and good humor.

To improve our outreach to the GTE workers, we once printed a survey we asked them to fill out and return to us by mail. To get surveys to as many workers as possible, one of us pushed the legal envelope a bit and stood across the street from the vigil beside the plant's driveway. None of us was sure if it was GTE property, but it did allow us more easily to pass material out to those drivers who had to stop anyway and were willing to open their windows.

Only four GTE workers responded.

One characterized our weekly vigil as "senseless" and said our religious acts of civil disobedience, like any action "that helps bring Communism closer," were "sacrilegious." As to how he or she would feel if GTE converted to non-military contracts, the person wrote, "It will never happen, thank God," and went on to say:

> Years ago, when we were the only country in the world that possessed nuclear weapons, we could have brought the entire world to its knees in a matter of days. That, however, is something that this God-fearing country could never do. On the other hand, if the Soviet Union had developed the atom bomb first, those of us who survived would now be speaking Russian . . . I will pray for the conversion of your souls.

Interestingly, that respondent did not acknowledge how, when we were the only country in the world that possessed nuclear weapons, we dropped them on two defenseless cities, incinerating over a hundred thousand men, women, and children.

Another worker, self-described as conservative and religious, said our vigil was "respectful, prayerful, and judgmental," while our religious actions were "wasted on most employees who actually agree with *most* of your ideals." Blocking traffic was called "antagonistic and less constructive than needed." He or she called us "judgmental, religious idealists." He or she believed the work at GTE made nuclear war less likely, and commented,

> You don't seem to understand that many employees here are anti-nuke and religious and concerned for a free and safe world . . . Please try to reach fresh minds, our government movers and shakers, the Soviet government. Inform them! Convince them, and I will lower my musket.

Like Eve when God asks her if she ate the forbidden apple, everyone tends blame others for wrongdoing. Eve points to Adam, who fingers the serpent. Arms workers, corporate executives, soldiers, politicians, voters, and taxpayers say anyone but them is responsible for evil. And so, unsurprisingly, the buck stops nowhere.

The third worker called the road-blocking civil disobedience "angering" and "counter-productive" and yet said they would be happy to see GTE convert to non-military contracts. They described themselves as a religious, liberal who couldn't find another job and didn't plan to work at GTE for long because of its military contracts. They went on to say, "Personally, I believe in your efforts to reduce military spending and avoid nuclear war. However, I don't always agree with methods which create tension and anger." Interestingly, the person suggested we would be more effective if we "speak the same language and dress in a manner which impresses others if you want them to listen."

I wasn't sure how to take the last remark, since our group were largely middle-class folks in conservative dress rather than long-haired, tie-dyed hippies.

The fourth respondent called our vigil prayerful and interesting. Feeling the company's work on the MX missile would not provoke nuclear war but help "win one for the Gipper," that person took a job a GTE because of salary and benefits, that person said,

> Please add my name to your mailing list, I am anxious to receive further literature about your organization and views, and to have a meaningful correspondence with you about issues of concern.

The most detailed insight into how workers felt about the Peace Witness at GTE didn't come to light until 2007 when an engineer named Barbara Roberts, who worked at GTE during most of the years of protest, gave an interview to Claire Schaeffer-Duffy. Entitled "Working on the Bomb." it ran in the April/May issue of *The Catholic Radical*. Barbara and her husband, Arthur, had, by 2007 become regular attendees of the weekly peace vigil in Worcester's Lincoln Square. She told Claire that GTE was not her first job choice but the first to offer work. She went on to say, "I don't think anybody at GTE wanted the missile fired or used. They wanted to be sure someone couldn't launch it by accident."

Claire wrote:

> According to Mrs. Roberts, many of her colleagues found the work psychologically taxing. Nuclear nightmares were common. One man dreamed of human body parts floating in water everywhere. Her boss, the son of a minister and a "very decent man" in his mid-forties, suffered from erratic blood pressure. There was a systems engineer who wrote poetry and naively believed nuclear war would be like any other—one side would win and take over. And the new hire who resigned after one day. And the humorist whose every joke related to nuclear war. She once asked him why he joked about such a topic, and he told her, "Because it scares the shit out of me."
>
> Roberts also had nightmares. In one dream, she was standing at a window on the north side of GTE looking west towards Worcester. Enormous black clouds were rolling across the whole earth towards her. "I just knew it was the end of the world," she said.
>
> When the protesters came, Mrs. Roberts and her colleagues would gather at the plant's upper windows and watch and discuss the scene below. After observing one demonstration, her friend, a female mathematician, turned and said with dismay, "They (GTE) are actually going to build the damn thing."
>
> Barbara concluded, "While you were working there, you didn't feel like you were working on a missile system. You didn't see the missile. You didn't see the warhead. You were dealing with pencil and paper requirements."

And yet, perhaps due in part to the protests, "people were disturbed by the project."

In a way, by breaking down the contract to construct global nuclear annihilation into many parts, each worker could deny individual responsibility. That attitude reminds me of a story of an inmate, lined up in a jail hallway, who feels a bump on his leg and hears, "Pass." When that happens a second time, he reaches down, and the inmate behind hands him a knife.

He in turn bumps the prisoner in front of him and says, "Pass." The process continues until an inmate far down the hall stabs another man to death. Although only one person did the bloody killing, it would not be possible without the collaboration of everyone in the line.

More directly, Pope John Paul I spelled out this reality in his poem:

The Armaments Factory Worker
I cannot influence the fate of the globe.
Do I start wars? How can I know whether I'm for or against?

No, I don't sin.
It worries me not to have influence.

I only turn screws, weld together
parts of destruction,
never grasping the whole or the
human lot.

I could do otherwise (would parts be
left out?),
contributing then to sanctified toil
which no one would blot out in
action or belie in speech.
Though what I create is all wrong,
the world's evil is none of my doing.

But is that enough?
And yet, judgment of others is always easy from the outside. We could label arms workers as naive, ignorant, delusional, nationalist, fundamentalist, militarist, or just plain selfish. After all, no matter how insidious the work at places like GTE, it's damned lucrative.

Scott and Claire Schaeffer-Duffy take their places at Saints Francis and Thérèse Catholic Worker in Worcester.
1990 photo by Christopher Navin in *Worcester Magazine*

But then, I recall a vignette from Aleksandr Solzhenitsyn's book *The Gulag Archipelago* where the author recalls the cruelty of guards nicknamed blue caps. Like the

Kapos, Jewish prisoners with some guard duties in Nazi concentration camps, the blue caps were inmate functionaries who, for minor privileges, oversaw other inmates. When the Soviet masters of the prison camp recruited Solzhenitsyn to become a blue cap, he accepted not for special treatment, but in order to show more mercy than others did.

To his surprise, though, Solzhenitsyn saw himself not displaying kindness but becoming crueler each day as a guard. Eventually, he resigned, concluding, "The line between good and evil runs not through states nor between classes nor between political parties, either—but right through every human heart."

Activists kid themselves if they believe they are more moral than those they protest. Most religions say that humanity is a family. People working at GTE are our brothers, sisters, mothers, fathers, sons, and daughters. We are cut from the same cloth. All of us lose our way at times. We are much more likely to find the path back to goodness if we don't feel devalued by critics.

In the book of Deuteronomy, God says, "I have set before you life and death, blessing and curse. Therefore, choose life that you and your descendants may live."

Undoubtedly, some people chose the dark side. Hitler, Stalin, and Walter F. O'Malley (owner of the Brooklyn Dodgers who moved the team to Los Angeles) for example, "chose poorly," to quote the guard at the climax of *Indiana Jones and the Last Crusade*, but no one is beyond redemption.

The Bible is loaded with stories of God selecting imperfect characters to be prophets. Moses had killed someone. Saint Paul hunted Christians down and oversaw their execution.

Barbara Roberts worked on a genocidal weapon system at GTE. Nonetheless, she became one of the most passionate and dedicated peace activists I've ever met. She was also a loving and cheerful person who cared about anyone in need.

The GTE campaign taught us that it is possible to help lift all boats. We might even be the final straw that breaks the back of injustice. Who knows?

But make no mistake, while the anti-MX campaign was significant, the nuclear arms race continued and continues still. *The Associated Press* reported on June 13, 2023, that

> The nine nuclear-armed states continue to modernize their arsenals, and several deployed new nuclear-armed or nuclear-capable weapons systems in 2022. Dan Smith, the director of the Stockholm International Peace Research Institute warned, "We are drifting into one of the most dangerous periods in human history."

The problem is so enormous and nuclear powers are so intractable, most people ignore the threat at the world's peril. How can anyone maintain a hopeful commitment to nuclear disarmament against such odds?

For me, the answer lies in Kurt Vonnegut's masterpiece, *Slaughterhouse-Five*, where the protagonist, Billy Pilgrim is "unstuck in time." At one moment, he finds himself a prisoner of war on a train to Germany in 1944, and then, without warning, he's a middle-aged optometrist in Illium, New York. Without warning, he is spirited in and out of dozens of episodes in his life, including his final moments.

In the novel, Pilgrim's experiences are not mere recollections. The scenes from his life are real. The benefit of the unusual phenomena is that Pilgrim is always aware of the other times. He understands suffering as temporary. Consciousness of joy diminishes the impact of suffering. Similarly, he relishes joy more deeply due to knowledge that it, too, is temporary.

The elation we experienced in that Worcester courtroom on All Saints Day in 1989 happened at that moment in history but continues to exist now and forever. Just as Christians consider Christ's death and resurrection events with cosmic significance, we can be buoyed by our own and other victories in the past.

Those triumphs actually occurred. Evil took a fall, and goodness won the day. We are not in LaLa land to believe that such things could happen again and that they are the inevitable destiny of humanity. The Book of Revelations talks about a future time when "every tear will be wiped away." Events like the jury verdict on November 2, 1989 give me hope to go on working for disarmament. That victory, like hundreds of thousands of others known and unknown in recorded history, is a reminder during a dark struggle that light can break through.

If we dispel the notion of time as linear, we can enter the space wherein Ken Synan had so much peace he could not hear the blah blah blah of GTE security or Westborough police. Like the great mystic Saint Teresa of Avila, we can say, "Let nothing disturb you. Let nothing frighten you. All things are passing away. God never changes. Patience obtains all things." With that conviction, we will not only persevere but will also be grace-filled at the hardest challenge we all must face, our own deaths.

I always wondered how some people managed witty or even humorous last words. After a long and painful illness brought him to death's doorstep, Oscar Wilde looked at the ugly wallpaper by his bed and said, "One of us has to go." When they laid his head on the chopping block, Sir Thomas More asked his executioner to move aside the long beard More had grown while jailed in the Tower of London because, "At least it has not offended the king." While being roasted alive on a hot griddle, Saint Lawrence reportedly said to his torturers, "Turn me over. I think I'm done on this side."

Humanity has done and continues to perpetrate atrocious things, but as horrible as we can be, we are also capable of acts so holy that they reverberate through time making divinity palpable and credible. As our evangelical friends say, "This train is bound for glory." Claire and I, along with many friends, family, and millions of other human beings, are doing our best to reserve tickets.

The Work Goes On

Members of the Atlantic Life Community were arrested at the UN after calling for nuclear disarmament on Ash Wednesday 2025. In August 2025 for the eightieth anniversaries of the atomic bombings of Hiroshima and Nagasaki by the United States, Claire Schaeffer-Duffy, Roman Catholic Archbishop John Wester of Santa Fe, and others joined a pilgrimage for disarmament to Hiroshima and Nagasaki.

The Atlantic Life Community and many other groups advocate for prevention of nuclear annihilation, climate catastrophe, deportation of migrants, and genocide of Palestinians.

In Blessed Memory

Ken Synan	1941-1992
Ellie Pepper	1933-1997
Bishop Tim Harrington	1918-1997
Bishop Bernie Flanagan	1908-1998
Dan Lawrence	1933-2001
Lillian Lamothe	1917-2002
Phil Berrigan	1923-2002
Ray Lamothe	1915-2005
Father Leo Barry	1925-2005
Tom Lewis	1940-2008
Peter DeMott	1947-2009
Father Bernie Gilgun	1927-2011
Connie Riley	1922-2011
Paul Giaimo	1962-2012
Father Dan Berrigan	1922-2016
Father Bob Branconnier	1925-2016
Doctor Ted Conna	1931-2016
Fremont Nantelle	1923-2019
Michael True	1933-2019
Bishop George Rueger	1929-2019
Margie Farren	1952-2020
Barbara Roberts	1942-2020
Sue Malone	1932-2021
Reverend Paul Ferrin	1929-2023
Tom Doughton	1948-2023

Tom Lewis

Margie Farren

Barbara Roberts

Michael True

Sue Malone

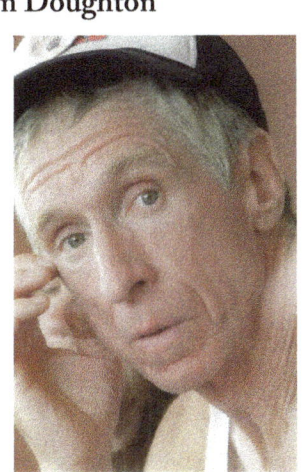

Peter DeMott

Father Bernie Gilgun

About the Author

Scott Schaeffer-Duffy holds a BA in religious studies from Holy Cross College, Worcester.

He is married to Claire Schaeffer-Duffy. They have four children and six grandchildren. They met at Catholic Worker communities in Washington, DC, where they were married in 1984. In 1986, they helped found the Saints Francis and Thérèse Catholic Worker house of hospitality for homeless men and women in Worcester, Massachusetts, where they continue to live and work.

Scott is the author of four other books: *Nothing Is Impossible: Stories from the Life of a Catholic Worker*, *Murder on Mott Street: A Catholic Worker Mystery*, *The Man Who Cannot Be Killed: A Catholic Worker Mystery*, and *Haunted: A Catholic Worker Mystery*.

Scott Schaeffer-Duffy

Scott welcomes all reader comments no matter the tone. Reach him by email at theresecw2@gmail.com and by regular mail at

Saints Francis & Thérèse Catholic Worker
52 Mason Street
Worcester, MA 01610

Colophon

Text for *Against All Odds* is set in Adobe Caslon Pro. Caslon is the name given to serif typefaces designed by William Caslon I (c. 1692–1766) in London or inspired by his work.

Caslon worked as an engraver of punches, the masters used to stamp the moulds or matrices used to cast metal type. He worked in the tradition of what is now called old-style serif letter design that produced letters with a relatively organic structure resembling handwriting with a pen. Caslon established a tradition of engraving type in London, which previously had not been common. His typefaces established a strong reputation for their quality and their attractive appearance, suitable for extended passages of text.

Caslon's typefaces were popular in his lifetime and beyond, and after a brief period of eclipse in the early nineteenth century, they returned to popularity, particularly for setting printed body text and books. Many revivals exist, with varying faithfulness to Caslon's original design. Modern Caslon revivals also often add features such as a matching boldface.

Titles for *Against All Odds* are sent in Bodoni, the name given to the serif typefaces first designed by Giambattista Bodoni (1740–1813) in the late eighteenth century and frequently revived since. Bodoni's typefaces are classified as didone or modern. Bodoni followed the ideas of John Baskerville, as found in the printing type Baskerville but he took them to a more extreme conclusion.

Bodoni had a long career, and his designs changed and varied, ending with a typeface of a slightly condensed underlying structure.

When first released, Bodoni and other didone fonts were called classical designs because of their rational structure. They came to be called modern serif fonts and then, until the mid twentieth century, they were known as didone designs. Bodoni's later designs are rightfully called modern, but the earlier designs are now called transitional.

www.ingramcontent.com/pod-product-compliance
Lightning Source LLC
Chambersburg PA
CBHW081841170426
43199CB00017B/2802